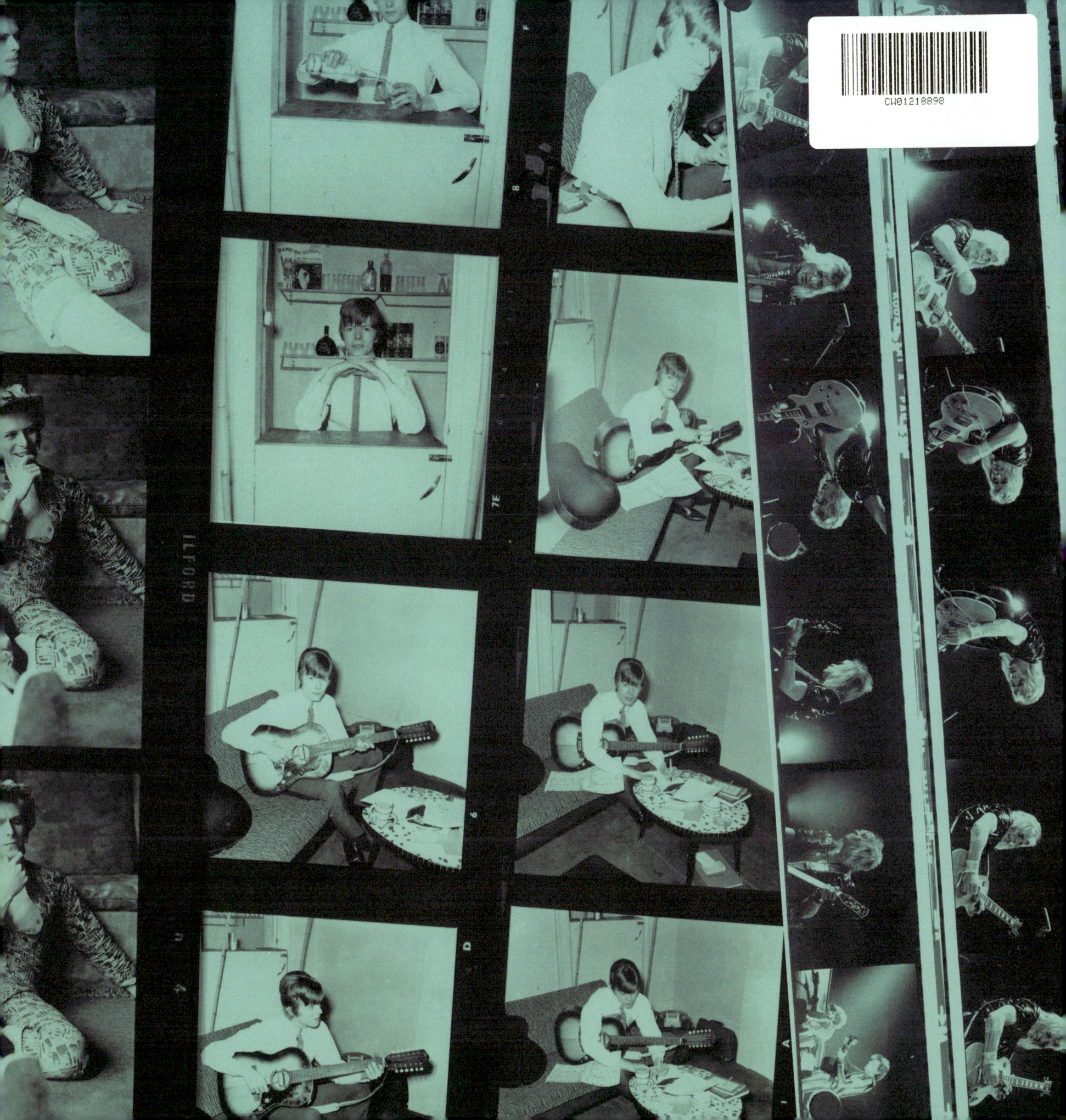

BOWIE
STARCHILD

Written by
Michael O'Neill

Danann
BOOKS

© Danann Publishing Limited 2016

First Published Danann Publishing Ltd 2016

WARNING: For private domestic use only, any unauthorised Copying,
hiring, lending or public performance of this book is illegal.

Photography courtesy of:
GETTY IMAGES;

Fiona Adams/Redferns
Potter / Stringer
Michael Ochs Archives / Stringer
Mark and Colleen Hayward
King Collection/Photoshot/Getty Images
RB/Redferns
Michael Putland
Debi Doss/Hulton Archive
Steve Wood / Stringer
Justin de Villeneuve/Hulton Archive
Terry O'Neill
Rob Verhorst/Redferns
GAB Archive/Redferns
Movie Poster Image Art

Michael Marks/Donaldson Collection
Beth Gwinn/Redferns
Richard McCaffrey/Michael Ochs Archive
Mark Sullivan/Contour
Peter Still/Redferns
Ron Galella/WireImage
Tony Mottram / Hulton Archive
Georges De Keerle
Bob King/Redferns
Brian Rasic / Hulton Archive
Frank Micelotta/ImageDirec
Dave J Hogan
Charlie Gillett Collection/Redferns

All other images Wiki Commons

Book layout & design Darren Grice at Ctrl-d

Copy Editor Tom O'Neill

All rights reserved. No Part of this title may be reproduced or transmitted in any material form (including photocopying or storing it in any medium by electronic means and whether or not transiently or incidentally to some other use of this publication) without the written permission of the copyright owner, except in accordance with the provisions of the Copyright, Designs and Patents Act 1988. Applications for the copyright owner's written permission should be addressed to the publisher.

Made in EU.
CAT NO: DAN0316
ISBN: 978-0-9931813-8-2

CONTENTS

- **4** — INTRODUCTION
- **6** — THE BOY WHO FELL TO BRIXTON 1947 - 1963
- **10** — YOU CAN CALL ME BOWIE 1963 - 1969
- **22** — A SPACE ODDITY 1969 - 1975
- **62** — SAVED IN BERLIN 1975 - 1979
- **80** — SO THIS IS SUCCESS 1980 - 1989
- **94** — CROSSING THE LINE 1990 - 1999
- **104** — THE GODS ARE HUMAN 1999 - 2004

BOWIE STARCHILD

INTRODUCTION

"David Bowie died on Sunday, two days after his 69th birthday."

It was a simple announcement repeated in every newspaper in the world in the early days of 2016, but it brought first shock and then tears to the eyes of generations of rock music aficionados who had followed and been profoundly affected by the fifty-year career and flamboyant lifestyle of one of popular music's most transcendent musicians.

The circumstances of his death were as noble and modest as his career had been glittering and superlative; his terminal illness had been a well-kept, 18-month long secret. The passing of David Bowie brought with it reminiscences of the disappearance of an age in which, for the first time, youth was assaulting and then destroying en masse the walls of restriction that had held them strapped onto their parents' notions of life. The revolutionary spinning turntables of rock in the 1950s and, the flower-power pollen of the 1960s were the catalysts that enabled the blossoming of Ziggy Stardust, and David Bowie became an iconic hero holding the flaming sword of self-expression aloft, fearlessly moving forwards onto uncharted territory, taking the search for the self to the next level. His uncompromising quest for personal freedom opened doors for countless numbers of people, who gladly followed his example and captured their own versions of personal freedoms. Perhaps, apart from a vague gnawing sense of dissatisfaction, they didn't know exactly what they were looking for; perhaps at the time, David Bowie didn't either, but in his relentless criss-crossing of boundaries and personalities that were applauded and idolised by millions, he freed the young restless and dissatisfied and assured them that different was not wrong; different was not inherently aggressive; different was simply frightening to those who had something to gain by confining others. This was an acknowledgment, a revelation that changed lives.

Yet, the enigma that was David Bowie has never been properly solved; the enigma of the man afraid and disdainful of restriction, dazzled by his own creations, sometimes owned by them, amazed by his own success; the man who crossed boundaries and married a Somali model, whose more conventional sensibilities could surely not have survived a lifetime of marriage to a man if his true character was as untouchable and ephemeral as the star-bound alter egos created for others to idolise.

Maybe Bowie's secret was the creation of such fantastical pop music creatures so divorced from the realities of life that they could be easily cast aside with the costumes once the stage door closed behind him even if the stardust in their wake almost brought about his personal armageddon.

Fans always wish to identify with their heroes by categorising them and squeezing out every ounce of their persona, almost wishing to morph into them. But Bowie refused to allow himself to be restricted by his fans, either. The performer kept them so mesmerised by his acting that they lost sight of the man slipping away from behind the masks.

WHERE, THEN, DID HE HIDE, THE MAN WHO WAS DAVID BOWIE?

THE BOY WHO FELL TO BRIXTON

In January 1947, Hayward Stenton Jones and his girlfriend Margaret Burns, Peggy, as she was known, lived in a very grey and deprived, austerity-wracked post-war Brixton in south London, at no. 40 Stansfield Road, awaiting Hayward's divorce from his wife so that they could marry. They were also awaiting something, or rather somebody, else; a little boy. He arrived eight months before the decree absolute did and was born at home on the 8th of January. His parents named him David Robert.

At the time, of course, David Robert didn't know that he would inherit a half-brother, Terence, born in 1937 from Peggy's pre-war relationship with a Jewish furrier. Nor did David know that he had a half-sister, Myra Ann given up for adoption after a wartime fling by his mother. Nor that there was a second half-sister, Annette, who his father had helped produce in 1941 during a wartime liaison with a waitress. Annette was raised by Hilda Sullivan, Hayward's ex-wife, and more or less vanished from David's timeline. Terence, on the other hand, had come to live with his mother and Hayward, and would generate his own headlines later in life, a victim of the Burns' family's *"mental instability"*. It may not be too far-fetched to attribute to David's aunts, who were by many accounts, missing a top floor, some contribution to the future life of David; perhaps his own demons were cleverly disguised by the creation of his future personas.

WHEN HAYWARD FINALLY BECAME FREE, HE AND PEGGY GOT MARRIED.

In 1951, David went to school, Stockwell Infant School. It's easy to imagine that the multi-coloured figures that populated his childhood in the Brixton area were nursemaids to the myriad character alternatives chosen by David in his later life. The dying embers of music hall could be found there, together with the failing characters that had once fed it; comedians, singers, dancers and illusionists were scattered like fading confetti in the streets around. The contrast to his mother's *"emotional restraint"* must have been extreme.

This rainbow broth amongst the bomb craters was abruptly withdrawn from his sight when the family moved to Bromley in Kent in 1954; to Plaistow Grove in suburbia and David's new school, Burnt Ash. Fortunately, Burnt Ash was forward thinking insofar as it stressed the importance of performing arts, music in particular, with pupils encouraged to dance out their feelings. The young David, slim and — crossing the gender barrier — sylph-like, developed the ability to captivate those around him, and one of those so captivated was the headmaster at Burnt Ash. Bright and dressed to perfection, David was the model image of a good boy, whose voice enhanced the Church of England choir that he joined; and what better teacher for theatrics and acting could he have had than the church, where dressing up entered his life in the shape of cassocks and ruffles for the set-piece stage performances that were church services and weddings.

It was the year 1955. It was the year rock 'n' roll cracked open David Jones' awareness of a new and unorthodox world inhabited by extraordinary people. Those people, brought *"... energy and colour and outrageous defiance"* into his life, and in the voice of little Richard, little David had heard the voice of God. This was the man David would idolise, the man whose sexual persona and glamour, whose flashy suits and flamboyance, even his later admission that he was gay, would prove to be the young Englishman's stepping stones along the yellow brick road to fame.

David was enraptured and longed to be in a band. He owned a ukelele. That didn't stop him and his friend George Underwood from going off to Scout camp in 1958 and putting together some songs, which George warbled around the camp fire to David's uke accompaniment.

There were more pressing questions for the young David, however, because aged 11, he had to choose a new school to attend. He ignored the grammar school and along with George, picked Bromley Technical College, which had links with Bromley College of Art in the building next door. Even here, David could spy adults dressing up as some of the teachers swished past in gowns and mortarboards.

The art department soon had David's rapt attention, and he explored his natural skill as an artist, but as time went on, his interest in the other subjects disintegrated until he was being labelled as a *"pleasant idler"* in his reports.

He and George continued to play music together, a subject about which David was fast becoming obsessive. As puberty set in, his interest expanded to take in girls – with no sign of latent or obvious homosexuality that he would later claim was part of his character. Hanging around in the record section of the local store, indulging his increasing taste for jazz, he would *"snog"* with the female assistant, who, at 17 years of age, was three years older than him. Before long, he was working at the local record store, a great place to attract the local girls. Whereas he described his attitude to girls as *"terrible"* they found him charming and *"nice"*.

Life for David was easy; his father indulged his whims and David could afford to sport a saxophone and dress in *"cool"* clothes which made him stand out, contemporaries remarking that he was noticed more for his appearance than his personality; there can be no doubt that the young David understood how useful this phenomenon could be and took the lesson that image overcomes everything, into his later career.

His life path, then, he was described as *"driven"* even at that young age,

RIGHT: Taken on Kingly Street, off Carnaby Street in summer 1963. Shoot for Boyfriend magazine with model who arrived with David

was slowly emerging; driven to the extent that he did not stop at double dealing even with his friend George, from whom he contrived to steal a girlfriend when the lads were both fifteen. How much of David's ruthless personality survived into the future we shall find out, but the immediate aftermath of the incident was an infuriated George, who smacked David in the head and managed, unintentionally, to scratch his eye. The injury to the iris muscles in David's left eye meant that it was unable to contract, so that the pupil was permanently dilated from then on, leading to the later confusion that he had two different coloured eyes.

Not long after, on June 12th 1962, George Underwood's band the Kon-Rads played at the PTA school fete at Bromley Tech. The group featured a saxophonist with a blonde quiff, David Jones, giving his first performance in public, looking well-dressed and cool as usual. No one thought for a moment that he had any chance of a music career, however. Except David, who although still out of the arena when the great bands of the era were springing up, was determined to be in the music business. He devoted his time to the band and his sax, even after a messy departure by George, to the detriment of his 'O' level work. To his chagrin, his attempts to change the band's musical direction and image failed, as did an audition with record producer Joe Meek, and their moment in the spotlight on the 'Ready Steady Win' talent show; won, incidentally, by a band with Peter Frampton as their guitarist.

David was growing impatient with his fellow band members as he continued to try and push them out onto unchartered territory where he felt they needed to be to get noticed. To no avail. So the sax player began to change things for himself. He announced that he was now calling himself David Jay. He wrote his own songs, one of which the band featured, called, **"I Never Dreamed"**.

Against the odds, by 1963, the chance of the big break arrived; a trial session for Decca Records. To David's dismay, this, too, turned into a dismal failure and it was one too many for the young and fiercely ambitious David Jay. His days with the band were over, he wanted to be involved in original material, as indeed, did George Underwood, and the two planned to form their own band.

David's 'O' level results were as bad as could have been expected; he failed them all except art. He could hardly have cared less, but now he had to get a job and the head of the school facilitated his start in life; employment at an advertising agency based in Yorkshire with an office in New Bond Street in London. Unsurprisingly, he hated the job of illustrator, with a passion. It was, however, a formative time; advertising, the art of presenting everything in a positive and glamorous light, of selling, often what no one knows they need, the art of attractive packaging, even of deception, formed David's thought patterns; another lesson learned. There was learning to be had, too, in Dobell's record shop, in the sounds of the blues or Bob Dylan.

George and David were inspired to change their band's name and now played gigs under the venerable tag, **"The Hooker Brothers"**. There was excitement in the musical air and George and David, eager to surf the rising wave, soon joined a new band, The King Bees. With them, David morphed into the lead singer, without much of a spark, according to contemporaries, and those who met him at the time were also lukewarm in their assessment of his off-stage character; *"very self-contained"*, *"likeable"* *"almost bland and boring in his single-mindedness"*, were some of the comments about the David Jay of those learning years, a young man self-confident in his flirtatiousness with both sexes. Author Paul Trynka wrote that David at seventeen seemed *"almost ruthless in his self-promotion"* and the word *"brash"* also rose to the surface. Perhaps only his humour saved him from stronger dislike by his peers; the realisation that charm was the way to the heart only arrived later.

THAT SINGLE-MINDEDNESS, THOUGH, WAS ABOUT TO PAY DIVIDENDS.

WITH A LITTLE HELP FROM DAD.

RIGHT: Bowie in pensive mood

THE BOY WHO FELL TO BRIXTON

BOWIE STARCHILD

YOU CAN CALL ME BOWIE

"Brian Epstein's got the Beatles and you should have us",

Trumpeted a letter that Hayward and David cooked up to persuade a British entrepreneur to dip his toes into the pop music industry and support The King Bees. Miraculously, the presumptuous froth in this letter ensured that it found its way through to a man who had been instrumental in the careers of such illustrious bands as The Shadows and The Bachelors, Leslie Conn. A scatterbrained and energetic charmer who had a razor-sharp eye for recognising talent, Les Conn invited the group to play in his living room. Perhaps David and George gave the performances of their lives, because now, the lead singer and his friend were described as possessing *"charisma"*.

Shortly afterwards, Conn was asking David's parents to co-sign a management contract, perhaps the first time that Peggy Jones saw any merit in her son's activities. She soon reverted to type, though, and grew tired of David's friends and lifestyle choices.

Conn sprang into action and drummed up gigs that included the famous Roundhouse in London's Camden Town, and set up a recording session at Decca. Absolutely convinced of his impending success, David Jay's first record, 'Louie Louie Go Home', a song by Paul Revere and The Raiders, was born in a studio in West Hampstead in London and featured 'Little Liza Jane' as the B-side. Set the music world on fire, it certainly did not.

David realised this very quickly, and this time, ruthless as ever, delivered a metaphorical blow to his friend George. In July 1964 he told George that he was leaving the band; he had found another one. Backstabbing his friend again, but David understood that in the music business it was often be brutal or die, and whatever else happened, David was not about to die. He had only taken the first step in his career, his voice was mediocre, but his ambition knew no bounds; he was going to be the number one.

The band that David had decided to join, even before they knew it themselves, was called the Manish Boys, an R&B outfit that was more than disappointed when they met their potential new singer, having assumed that he was black. David's suave appearance swung the initial meeting in his favour as did the fact that he wrote his own songs and confidently

RIGHT: 3rd March 1965: Portrait of the then Davy Jones

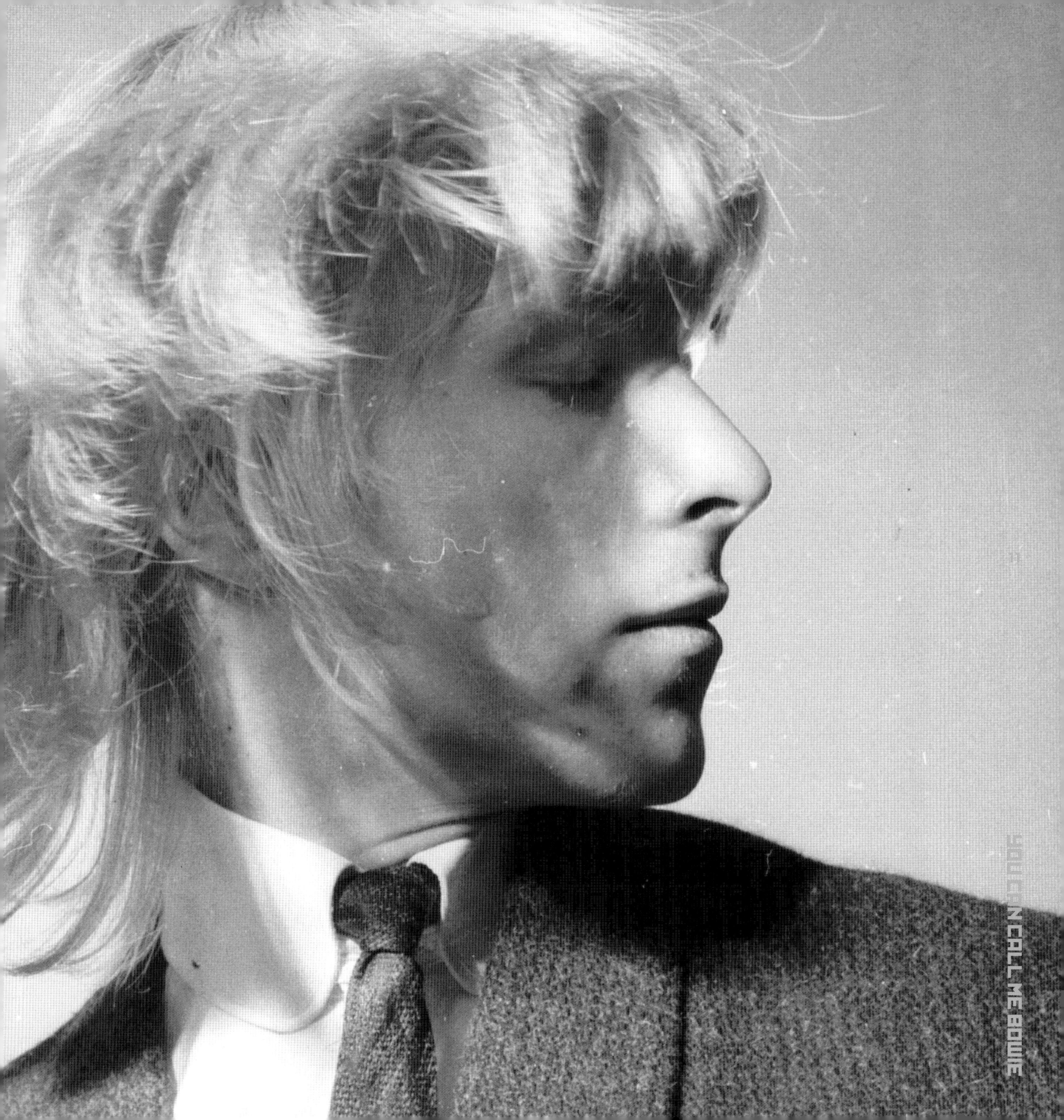

BOWIE STARCHILD

suggested new material. One month later, Davie was out on the road with his new band. And the unformed voice in the unusual, slim singer began to generate the undivided attention of audiences from the start. Using his own English accent, David started to understand how he could use the microphone to increase the effect of his delivery of a song, and his vocal approach improved. Almost unnoticed, David's influence altered the band's music, their appearance, their performance style. David Hadfield, Bowie's band mate in the Kon-Rads, acknowledged his friend's greatest contribution to the group; his ideas. *"He had thousands of them, a new one for every day – that we should change the spelling of our name, or our image, or our clothes."*

Bowie also wheeled out endless advertising campaign designs, acutely aware of the magnetic power of suggestion and image.

FINALLY, THE KID FROM BROMLEY WAS ABLE TO FILL OUT THE SKETCHES OF HIS MUSICAL AND ARTISTIC DREAMS.

Having resigned from his job at Nevin D. Hirst Advertising, David threw himself with carefree abandonment into the lifestyle that was the birthright of every nascent pop musician of the 1960's. His sexual appetite was said to have been as insatiable as it was indiscriminate, and flirting came a long way ahead of the task of packing away the band's equipment after a gig. And he cannot have failed to understand the implications – personal and professional – buried in the fact that most of the lipstick messages left on the band's van were for him.

Les Conn decided to hand the band over to the capable hands of Mickie Most, who wanted to work with them at their very first meeting together. It was September 1964.

AND THE BAND FLUNKED THEIR OPPORTUNITY.

Which did nothing to dent David's confidence whatsoever. And his confidence seemed to be well founded, because the band was soon booked to play at the legendary Star Club in Hamburg. The story, according to David, was that he had told the club's promoter that he was gay, implying that this confession had swung the gig in their favour. Whether this was true, an example of David doing whatever was necessary to promote his career, or David burnishing his own flighty image simply for the benefit of those around him, we shall never know.

Les Conn was still proving his worth, and after arranging a package tour deal for the band, he persuaded American producer Shel Talmy to listen to David; and Talmy was impressed by what he heard. So The Manish Boys were ushered into the studio to record a cover version of **"Pity the Fool"** on January 15th 1965. David's performance was polished, brimming with confidence, although his talent as a songwriter was somewhat lacking as the B-side of the single, **"Take My Tip"**, his first recorded song, showed.

Nonetheless, with Talmy enthusiastic about the blonde singer, it seemed as though they were on their way.

Unexpectedly, everything derailed. The single vanished, the gigs in Hamburg followed suit and the gigs in England began to make themselves scarce, too. Arguments flared about who should have top billing and about finances, and to top it all, the group's van gave up the ghost. The Manish Boys were strangling themselves. As the group went through its death throes, George Underwood's musical career was flourishing and David could not help but let his jealousy bubble to the surface. When David, having, as usual, taken off with a female groupie, failed to reappear after a gig, the band and its singer unceremoniously fell apart at the seams.

David auditioned for yet another group, The Lower Third, and although his voice was still far from being the best in the business, it was his image that pulled him through. And once again, it was David Jones who took the driving seat, pushing the band to learn new songs. And, once again, the advertising was designed by Jones and would declare that there was a new group on the scene known as, **"Davie Jones and The Lower Third"**. David had found the springboard he had wanted and he now concentrated all of his energies into making the band the success that he so craved. He also craved songwriting success, but by all accounts his efforts in this direction were fairly dire, producing nothing but pale shadows of a host of already popular singers. Undaunted, he continued writing.

David and the band entered that summer in buoyant mood, enjoying one another's company on and offstage and fulfilling a series of gigs in south-east England. But obstacles were bubbling to the surface. Les Conn had fallen out of love with the music business and with pushing David and another of his protégés, later to become Marc Bolan, without success. He decided to call it a day. Around the same time, Shel Talmy cancelled the singles deal with David after pressure from EMI, who felt that David was simply not yet ready for the big time. By which time David had lined up a replacement for Les Conn in the shape of Ralph Horton, who was then in his late 20s and became devoted to

BOWIE STARCHILD

furthering David's career. The fly in the ointment was Horton's jagged relationship with the other members of the band. Horton was enamoured with David, jealous of him and conspired to separate him from his band, luring him away into his car for travel to gigs leaving the band to travel alone.

And David had become aware of another problem; there already was a singer called David Jones, and he was soon to become extremely famous as part of The Monkees. The other David Jones decided to use a name he had toyed with ever since his time in the Kon-Rads when he had become obsessive about a fictional character played by the actor Richard Widmark; Jim Bowie, a true American pioneer, whose biography mixes reality with legend, fearlessness and adventure. David had found his role model, and his next and most important transformation to date took place; it broke with the past, it pointed the way to a glittering future borne aloft by a name that signified glamorous courage in the face of the unknown; David Bowie was born.

Bowie has been quoted as saying at the time, **"When I'm famous, I'm not gonna speak to anybody – not even the band."** His sense of his own destiny his own unique importance was obvious even then, although he put it on the back burner for the glorious summer of 1966, when Horton had his boys travelling from gig to gig, on stage with bands such as The Who, and playing at the top of their game.

Bowie, not a natural songwriter at the time, kept writing although putting his words to music was like squeezing blood from a stone. One of the themes that he came up with concerned the sharply dressed and pill-popping boys known as Mods, who Ray Davies had immortalised. Narcissism was a badge of honour amongst the 1960s Mods, and David Bowie and Marc Bolan gravitated to the top of the pile. Bowie's song was called 'The London Boys', and in it, he was laying the foundation stones of the persona that would emanate the naive world-weariness that Bowie would claim as his second skin for another decade. Coupled with his androgynous looks and eternally boyish figure, Bowie had found the face he would turn to the world, just as Charlie Chaplin had once found his. And the Mods were surrounded by an air of latent homosexuality; many of them tried out sexual partners of both genders, and David, described by one male friend who **"fell in love"** with him, as **"semi-straight, semi-gay"**, was a natural addition to the Mod scene. In this London where appearances mattered, the truth was a moveable feast. Mostly, David preferred the girls to the boys and flaunted his camp behaviour more as bait for the females than the men. But it was good a marketing move to court both sides of the divide and David did it to perfection.

Horton now delivered his coup; he negotiated a recording contract with producer Tony Hatch. Not overly impressed with David, Hatch was, nonetheless, astute enough to realise that, in the right hands, David had a career ahead of him, although he didn't anticipate short-term success. David also had a lot of songs to show, one of which was **"Can't Help Thinking about Me"**, which, although elements were plagiarised, demonstrated that David's work on his composing techniques had borne fruit. Hatch thought the single was **"standout"** and it was released on the 14th January 1966. Nineteen-year-old Bowie was convinced that the door had swung open.

NOT QUITE.

The record failed to gain entry into the Record Retailer Top 40, London's premier pop record chart. It did rise to number 25 in Radio London's favourites, and Bowie was excited, anyway.

And yet, at the moment when that elusive temptress success seemed to be temptingly close, everything collapsed around Bowie once more. Horton had successfully managed to cocoon David in a world of their own away from the band. He spent money recklessly and left the band financially desperate. The inevitable split was not long in coming, and when the band refused to play one gig unless they were paid, the dream was over. David always felt that he owed allegiance only to himself, and he chose to stay with Horton; the other band members went their way without him. It turned out to be a bad move for David, because the band that Horton then formed to back his singer, The Buzz, lacked the

LEFT: Portrait by Robin Bean, London, 1967

coherent expertise of The Lower Third musicians.

Bowie's next single, **"Do Anything You Say"** was flat and uninspired. Derailed by his own manager, Bowie without The Lower Third floundered in a musical soup, lacking direction, unable to find the guiding star of his own musical ambitions. This period when he lacked focus, when his own self-interest had blown him off course, embarrassed Bowie to the extent that he later photoshopped it from his autobiography, banning it to the hinterland of vague generalisations. Keeping what he considered to be the unpalatable parts of his autobiography from public view was something that he always tried to do, encouraging everyone around him, for example, to believe that he was an only child; a half-truth used as a get-out clause.

Anyone who knows Bowie's character can only conclude that the way he acted at that time was inevitable; he was a loner, his interest was in himself and his fantasies, which were driven by the desire to escape the stifling, conventional, repetitive boredom of life with his parents. To be with Bowie was to listen to his flights of fantasy, his plans for his future. He was fortunate that many people found the combination of his reed-like figure and childish enthusiasm intriguing and allowed him to act as he pleased. One of those people, of course, was Ralph Horton.

Horton was aware that at this low point in Bowie's career, his protégé was likely to strike a deal with someone else and leave his manager mourning in his wake. With this in mind, Horton persuaded the music manager Ken Pitt to watch Bowie at work.

What happened at this audition gig has become mired in myth and subjected to the smoke and mirrors that appeared whenever Bowie was near. Suffice it to say that Pitt saw enough in Bowie to invite him for a long talk and was then impressed by the young man's bright-eyed enthusiasm. So David had a new manager, one who would exert a profound influence on the singer. Pitt gave his new acquisition the width of freedom that he desired, supported his extrovert persona, encouraged him to wear make up and, above all, to write more songs.

Armed with new songs, David went back into the studio for a session funded by Pitt, who was excited by the new material so unlike anything he had known. And Hugh Mendl, an executive at Decca, was of the same opinion when Pitt sent the songs to him. Mendl went into reveries when talking about David, commenting that he found him **"the most talented, magical person"**. David, it seems, had perfected the art of dazzling those around him with light, his equivalent of the American mantra **"fake it till you make it"**, although not everyone – one of Decca's producers, Mike Vernon, who would guide the first album to life, being one of them – was convinced of the genius behind the gossamer rainbow persona. But even he was delighted with the river of creativity that this new singer was tapping into.

His backing band The Buzz had faded from David's new life as he wrote song

RIGHT: David Bowie poses for a portrait session on a proof sheet in 1966 in London

after song for the proposed album, entitled simply, **"David Bowie"**. Trying for a new orchestral sound but not knowing how to read music, Bowie engaged bassist Dek Fearnley to get the arrangements into shape. It seems that everyone got carried away with Bowie's unfocused inventive chaos and use of the studio as an instrument in itself, and Bowie confessed later that he was being carried along in a torrent of influences from Anthony Newley to music hall.

Some of the tracks were, in a word, awful. Some were fun to make for those involved. What eventually emerged was something that writer David Buckley called **"the vinyl equivalent of the madwoman in the attic"**. Enough said. Predictably the record failed to urge anything but mild comment anywhere, though Penny Valentine of 'Disc' magazine expressed her positive views on his talent – and was thus subjected to a torrent of phone calls from Bowie. In later years, hindsight showed that the seeds of Bowie's major themes and personas could be found ghosting around the texts of the album. True to form, failure was the mad aunt in the attic for Bowie, and the singer himself would never speak of the album again.

Now twenty-one years old, Bowie was about to experience another change, leaving home. For a boy who was so dismissive of suburban boredom and parental oversight he had found he much preferred to be looked after than look after himself. But his half-brother Terry, who as David discovered, suffered from schizophrenia, had returned to the fold after National Service in the RAF. The little house was overcrowded and David moved in with Ken Pitt, who took over the role of paymaster general for his fledgling singer.

Pitt it seems, had also fallen under the spell of the uncultured, as he described him, elf prince, indulged the naked frolics of his singer and reciprocated, but refused to be drawn on the question of Bowie's homosexuality, imagined or otherwise, wisely realising he was treading on dangerous ground for himself. Pitt took over the father figure role and added to Bowie's natural curiosity in the world around him, continuing the cultural further education that he had started to give him by taking Bowie to the theatre and encouraging him to read literature. This was, it seems, an enjoyable time for both men.

But what Bowie really needed more urgently was to find his own musical style and pair it with the ability to write interesting songs. He was still writing; in fact, the songs were piling up in Ken's flat, but even when the songs were farmed out to other groups they failed to

BOWIE STARCHILD

set anything alight. His best effort was **"Let Me Sleep Beside You"**, which, in collaboration with producer Tony Visconti, became a delicious piece of music. But it still couldn't break the deadlock. Bowie continued to hang around with little prospect of success. The weeks turned into months of inactivity and his confidence began to pay the price. He was succumbing to depression, and previously unthinkable thoughts began to pray on his mind; perhaps he should finally give up. After all, Pitt was having no success in trying to sell his protégé to producers, film producers or commercial agents.

Ironically, failure, the word that Bowie denied access to his autobiography, proved to be the making of him.

In 1968, and in the middle of this disturbing era of doldrums, serendipity knocked at the door. She was to lead David down a path towards a style of performance that would leave its indelible mark on the rest of his career. Sitting in the vacuum of his stalled career, David was invited to see a performance by actor, dancer and mime artist Lindsay Kemp. Kemp had listened to Bowie's album and professed himself **"absolutely enchanted"** by what he had heard, and he used one of the songs to open his show 'Clowns'; hence the invitation to David.

It was a meeting of kindred spirits, **"love at first sight"**, as Kemp said following his meeting with the singer, noting a **"plaintive, damaged"** quality to Bowie's voice that attracted him at first. With Kemp steeped in enthusiasm for all things theatrical from Japanese Kabuki to the Theatre of the Absurd, it also was humour and a shared delight in music hall, it seems, that kept Kemp's interest in the young visitor alive. Bowie had met his second mentor, who was also his lover – according to Kemp – and teacher. **"I taught him to express and communicate through his body"**, says Kemp. **"I taught him to dance"**.

And he taught him something vital that would bring all of it together; the importance of **"the look – makeup, costume, general stagecraft, performance technique"**.

Kemp fed the youngster with books to read and pictures to absorb. He spoke about Kabuki, and the avant-garde. Now the Tibetan Society became one of Bowie's ports of call and was coupled with an introduction to the colours of mysticism. The music scene also floated along in a fug of dope smoke and mysticism, and Bowie, willing to partake in any interesting experience, was happy to take his drag of any spliffs going. There were meditation sessions with friends that drew on Tibetan Buddhism – and although David's chameleon-like character could never settle on any one direction for his life, he had devoted time to the study of Buddhism, and his interest was serious. Fascinated by the bohemianism, the outcasts of the 'respectable' world that accumulated in Kemp's flat, Bowie fell in love with the alternative lifestyle he found that was so opposed to anything he had lived with his parents. He had been shown his niche, his way forward out of the musical impasse.

Kemp and David were soon planning a new show together, 'Pierrot in Turquoise'. Now David could be found attending dance lessons at Kemp's Floral Street studio. He wasn't a natural, but Kemp encouraged him to express with his body what was hidden inside, and the singer was a willing pupil.

Bowie's character was named Cloud, a singing and speaking modern variant of a Greek chorus rolled into one person, and wearing makeup and costume for the first time, he began to write songs for the show, which saw the light of day in Oxford and then went on tour.

"I cringe when I see it now", says Kemp, **"it was so naive"**.

Still, Bowie produced 'Columbine', considered one of his finest songs of the time, along with a variety others that showed he was moving in a coherent direction. The show also proved that Bowie was as fickle as ever; Kemp apparently discovered his lover in bed with the

RIGHT: Portrait of David Bowie photographed in 1967

YOU CAN CALL ME BOWIE

BOWIE STARCHILD

show's costume designer Natasha. But as Kemp, no retiring wallflower himself, was only too aware, that's showbiz. Natasha was soon replaced by Hermione Farthingale, a classically trained dancer who David had worked with in a BBC drama, **"The Pistol Shot"**, early in 1968. She, quieter more reflective and intellectual, and David, the constant joker, were enraptured with one another and their relationship had a positive, even transformative, effect on Bowie. The tensions of the past months eased away and he began to enjoy life again.

In August that year he moved again, this time to live with Hermione in an attic room in a house in South Kensington, which she shared with several other people. And there, for the next six months, Bowie was content to be rocked in the cradle of bourgeois life surrounded by elegance and comfort, and the few new songs he wrote during that time reflect this.

The relationship seemed to have dissolved much of his arrogant aggression, made him happier in his skin; but he was aware that his career was treading water, and his friend Marc Bolan's increasing success was in stark contrast to his own flatlined career. To earn money, he began working at a photocopy shop close to the High Court in London

Ken Pitt had been relegated to a figure on the periphery of David's life, now centred on Hermione and life in South Kensington, and it was with Hermione and guitarist Tony Hill that he put together a *"multimedia"* trio that went by the name of Turquoise. They put on a show at the Roundhouse in Camden, but Hill left after the second performance. It was his old bandmate from The Buzz, John Hutchinson, who came to the rescue. Back from Canada, Hill had brought new musical ideas for Bowie to absorb; the sounds of Leonard Cohen or Joni Mitchell. Bowie, through the singer songwriter and sometime Bowie-lover Lesley Duncan, had also discovered iconic French chansonnier Jack Brel. Brel songs found their way into the performances of the new line up of Feathers, which was a potpourri of dance, poems and songs, tape recordings and mime. The troupe was destined not to last for long, and provided, at best, a hiatus in which David became more centred.

Money problems arose, the couple were living hand to mouth and neither Hermione nor David had any career to speak of. And suddenly, Hermione was passing up the line in auditions for a feature film. Bowie dreaded what her success would mean, and there were tensions as the relationship slowly unravelled.

Change was coming, Bowie could sense it, sense that he was losing the idyllic life he had led with Hermione, was about to be cut loose from the 'oasis' they inhabited; but he had no idea that his doodling around on his Stylophone was the key to opening the door to his musical future. Bowie began to write a song, which he set out like a piece of theatre, and the ethereal chords he produced created a sense of space and wistfulness.

When he and John had finished work on the piece, which had a musical structure all of its own, Major Tom was ready to float to fame in 'Space Oddity'. Having absorbed of all the multi-coloured influences of his life and filtered them through his own creative inventiveness and current emotional turmoil, he had finally produced something unique. A simple theme was held up by a complex musical construct, the gradations of music mirrored the lyrics, the harmonic structures moulded the atmosphere, the theme of disconnected isolation encapsulated the essence of Bowie's view of himself, even though it was inspired by the film **"2001: A Space Odyssey"**.

One door closed as another, the one that David had longed to see swing wide for so long, finally allowed him access to fame and fortune, the mistress he had ruthlessly courted and to whom he would be enslaved for the rest of his life. Adoration was the singer's lifeblood as necessary for his music as a guitar.

NOW SHE WAS HIS.

RIGHT: Posed studio portrait of David Bowie, 1969

YOU CAN CALL ME BOWIE

Hermione walked out. To Norway to shoot her film, and she ejected Bowie from her life. How far away was the precious time they had spent together, when she thought of him as lovely, sweet and kind. How glad she must have been that she had held back from marrying him when they were thinking of tying the knot; Bowie's behaviour – the chauvinism that demanded ironed shirts and meals on the table, the insatiable promiscuity – eventually proved too much even for her tolerant and placid nature. The break-up was to leave him in tears back at his parents' house and trigger a downward slide into cocaine abuse and the instant gratification of casual sex. Nevertheless, Hermione respected Bowie and their time together and refused to speak about it afterwards.

Bowie was on the ropes and were it not for the card up his sleeve — 'Space Oddity' — who can tell where his future would have taken him.

It didn't take him long to replace Hermione with Mary Finnegan. He was living with her and her children within two weeks of their first meeting. As a writer for the International Times, Mary took up the cudgels on behalf of her wavering lover. It was she who set up what came to be known as the Beckenham Arts Lab at the Three Tuns Pub where David centred his activities amongst poets and puppeteers, musicians and artists. Bowie dabbled with the hippie movement and sang his songs amidst this collection of artistic outsiders and their audiences.

Around this time in 1969, Calvin Lee, who David had met in 1967, became Head of Promotions for Chappell Music Publishers. He was one of the satellites that rotated adoringly around David Bowie and for a short time he was his lover, though the brevity of the relationship made Lee wonder if Bowie was attempting his own version of sleeping his way to the top. Lee was impressed with the alien atmosphere of 'Space Oddity' and did all he could to promote it and David, encouraging Simon Hayes, Head of International A&R at Mercury, to sign the singer, which is what eventually happened.

By May 1969, Bowie had found another woman to champion his cause; her name was Angela Barnett, a feisty American, who would not only become deeply involved in Bowie's career, she would also become the wife of the **"alley cat"**, as she described him.

David was fortunate in that he had created his single just before the Apollo moon landing was due to take place, and it was this event that made what everyone considered to be a good song, into a marketable one. Even though producer Tony Visconti disliked the song at the time, he, too, saw the opportunity and began planning a follow-up album; everything needed to happen quickly before the Apollo launch.

RIGHT: Bowie plays an acoustic Espana 12-string guitar to promote the release of his album 'Space Oddity' in November 1969

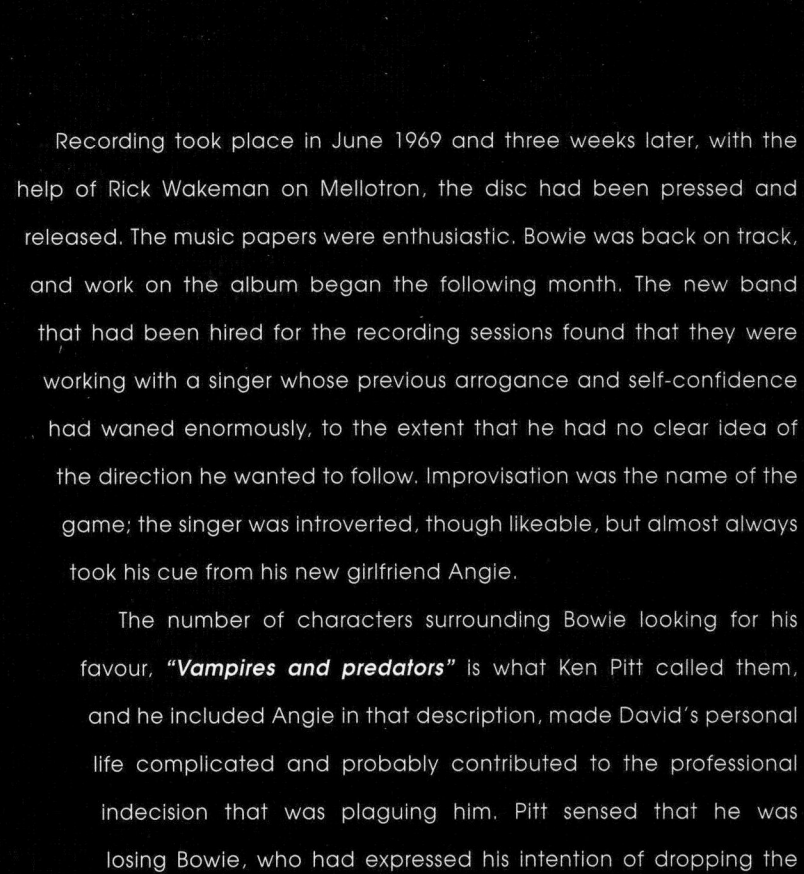

Recording took place in June 1969 and three weeks later, with the help of Rick Wakeman on Mellotron, the disc had been pressed and released. The music papers were enthusiastic. Bowie was back on track, and work on the album began the following month. The new band that had been hired for the recording sessions found that they were working with a singer whose previous arrogance and self-confidence had waned enormously, to the extent that he had no clear idea of the direction he wanted to follow. Improvisation was the name of the game; the singer was introverted, though likeable, but almost always took his cue from his new girlfriend Angie.

The number of characters surrounding Bowie looking for his favour, *"Vampires and predators"* is what Ken Pitt called them, and he included Angie in that description, made David's personal life complicated and probably contributed to the professional indecision that was plaguing him. Pitt sensed that he was losing Bowie, who had expressed his intention of dropping the manager after the record was released, anyway, and sent his singer off to take part in two continental song festivals in Malta and Italy in August. Shortly after Bowie arrived home, he received the message that his father was seriously ill, suffering from pneumonia. On the 5th of August, Hayward died. The news hit David very hard. His father would surely have been wonderfully proud of the success of the son he had done so much to support through so many difficult times.

As if to intensify the vortex of conflicting emotions in which David found himself, **"Space Oddity"** entered the UK charts in September 1969 at number 48, and then, like Major Tom, it slipped away into space. And had it not been for Olav Wyper, the new general manager of Phillips, that may well have been that. When Olav discovered the promotion, marketing and sales staff sitting around twiddling their thumbs one-day, he set the entire team to work on **"Space Oddity"**. Thanks to Wyper, before the month was out, the single was back in the chart at

BOWIE STARCHILD

number 25 and eventually hit number 5.

In November the album 'Space Oddity' was released, but the clash of personalities between producers, managers and Bowie's wife, ensured that it only came sneaking out as though it were ashamed of itself. Unfortunately, Olav Wyper found the album forgettable.

"I was looking for myself", was the singer's admittance of the album's weaknesses. There was no coherence, no convincing view of his world to propel the lyrics and music forward, and David himself seemed to be thrashing around ineffectually. All was not well.

Still, for the time being, with the 'Space Oddity' single bringing in a steady trickle of royalties and its success enabling him to raise his fees for live concerts, David had his own money at his disposal for the first time in his life - and he spent it as though it grew in flowerpots. He and Angie moved into Haddon Hall in Beckenham in September 1969 where Angie, educated in Switzerland at a British boarding school, unstoppably loud and energetic, extended her sovereignty over David. Angie would later say that when she fell **"hopelessly in love"** with David, she realised that to him she was primarily **"a nurse, cook, housekeeper, creative ally and business adviser"**. Haddon Hall also became a home to some of David's friends, and whatever else she was, Angie was an excellent hostess, and the residents and their friends, such as drummer John Cambridge, would celebrate **"exuberant"** parties. And David wrote a love song to her, **"the Prettiest Star"**, in such a conventional style that it's almost unique amongst Bowie's works.

It was 1970, and David was now 23 years old. Ken Pitt was being quietly sidelined, and David's brother Terence had been admitted to a psychiatric hospital, the same one that had housed Charlie Chaplin's mother, Cane Hill in Croydon, London. Terence could now be seen at Haddon Hall, too, although eventually, Terry's schizophrenia would prove too daunting for David to cope with. Fearful of the mental instability in his family, the singer felt guilty and adrift when faced with his half-brother's problems, and although he appeared outwardly calm about the situation, the emotional drag exercised by Terry found its way into Bowie's songs.

With a BBC **"In Concert"** session lined up, Bowie found himself having to put together a backing group. His friend John Cambridge

LEFT: Bowie poses for a portrait smoking a cigarette to promote the release of his 'Hunky Dory' album in December 1971

was an obvious choice for drummer, and he persuaded Bowie to take on guitarist Mick Ronson, who had developed his own unique playing style. The third in the trio was producer Tony Visconti, who volunteered to play bass, and the group went through two names, Harry the Butcher, and then David Bowie's Imagination, before being reincarnated as The Hype.

When Cambridge left in April 1970, he was replaced by Mick **"Woody"** Woodmansey, and they were all joined in November that year by Benny Marshall, on vocals and harmonica. The group proved highly influential and is credited with being instrumental in the birth of Glam Rock. The BBC concert itself, with the band only having been so recently put together, stumbled a bit, but everyone knew that an exciting moment had arrived. Bowie felt the creative juices flowing through his veins again, and the interval between the BBC concert and a planned gig at London's Roundhouse was filled with Ronson and Bowie's creativity as they let the ideas flow at Haddon Hall. In the meantime, Angie went searching for theatrical costumes for the musicians; David was given a flowing multi-coloured concoction. It was Angie who encouraged Bowie to be outrageous, and in doing so she opened another career door for him to pass through.

The Roundhouse concert was remembered for being a bit of a mess, but it was the moment when David began to ease into his new persona, away from the unfocused wavering of previous years. Egged on by Ronson's powerful guitar, David began to move his body in ways he had learned from Lindsay Kemp and he seemed to be relaxed and enjoying the freedoms offered by this new world.

On the face of it, this new world also held the prospect of a long-term relationship with Angie, and in March, she and David got married at Bromley register office; despite the fact that he had, apparently, told her before they got married that he didn't love her. But their marriage, she said, was an open relationship from the very beginning, and she thought that she could cope with it. However, she would see swathes of men and women make offers to David to the point where, she says, it almost became overwhelming. Later, she would claim that David used sex as a tool to achieve his professional ambitions, charming people into liking him and then loving him, so that they would be emotionally charged to work hard at his career. This was life with Bowie and you either signed up for the deal or you weren't in the club. Even the night before their marriage they were said to have indulged in a threesome, and they closed the matrimonial ceremony with a drink in the local pub.

The marriage withstood the blows for 10 years; the death throes would be nasty, and in typical Bowie style, Angie followed in a long line of perceived failures that he photoshopped from his interview autobiography.

For the time being, though, Angie was a force to be reckoned with around Bowie and was a positive influence in many ways.

With another album recording in preparation, David was more determined than ever to take Ken Pitt out of the equation and had meetings with lawyers and accountants, Tony Defries and Laurence Myers, to try to extricate himself from his contract. Pitt suspected that this was going to happen at some point, anyway. Nonetheless, the final meeting with the singer and these men floored him. He felt hurt and betrayed; had he not promoted and financed Bowie during a period when no one else would? There was nothing to be done; the relationship was over.

Recording began in April with the new drummer Mick Woodmansey, and Bowie appeared more confident than in the past, although still strangely unassertive, and the finished album seems to have been filled with the creative input of Tony Visconti rather than Bowie. When the singer was absent, which was often, Ronson and Visconti were working on completing songs, and the aggressive guitar brilliance of Ronson seemed to inspire Bowie to dig deeper into the distortions of dark themes. One of those touched on in the track 'All the Madmen', was insanity, and with Terry in Cane Hill, it possesses a terrible poignancy as the music moves from quirky fragility to heavy rock. And this phenomenon recurs throughout Bowie's career; the singer made greater through the contribution of others, which was enabled and ennobled, in turn, by the singer. 'The Man Who Sold the World' was delivered by a Bowie connecting his very

BOWIE STARCHILD

personal singing style with all the years of musical influences and finally merging them to make a coherent, simple, but emotionally saturated whole.

By May, the album had been mastered only for Bowie to discover that his champion at the Philips record company, Olav Wyper was being replaced. And there was more devastating news to come. Once again, when seemingly on the cusp of breaking through the barriers, his supporters deserted him; Tony Visconti and Mick Ronson walked out, Tony left Haddon Hall and switched his attention to Marc Bolan, and before a new single, 'Holy Holy' was released, 'Woody' Woodmansey was no longer around, either. 'Holy Holy' was released at the beginning of 1971 and vanished in a puff of smoke. Bowie, it seemed, was an acquired taste that no one wanted to acquire. His new manager, Tony Defries, was far more interested in getting hold of Stevie Wonder than promoting David Bowie and found David's neediness, which manifested itself in constant phone calls, tiresome in the least. And he still had to sit out the expiration of Bowie's old contract. Bowie was truly alone, with his career stalling and only Angie still standing at his side.

And it was Angie who kept him afloat in every sense, tending to all of his demands and desires, sucking up to the management team, drawing Bob Grace of Chrysalis into their world — though he wondered why they seemed constantly obsessed with the gay scene — planning and scheming, Bowie's very own personal Machiavelli. With no other choice, no other musical collaborators to lean on, no one to draw support from, Bowie took to working out songs, painstakingly, on an old upright piano that he had acquired. It was there, he said later, that with hard, hard work, he had forced himself to become a good songwriter. He had to replace natural talent with a steep learning curve. The piano provided a fresh start, a new way to approach songs and he incorporated elements from all of his musical heroes, from all musical traditions that he had encountered and built the innovative musical landscape he had always wanted. His sex life was as ambiguous as ever, and he encouraged misinterpretations alongside correct impressions as to his sexual orientation because they lent him a risqué, rather louche persona that would draw a line between normalcy and how he wished to be perceived.

The only movement to his career at this time came in the form of a promotional tour of America for 'The Man Who Sold the World' album. Not that the album had done well in America, it hadn't at all. But as usual, David had a saucer-eyed fan, in the guise of Ron Oberman, press officer at Mercury in America. Angie was pregnant, so David was footloose and

RIGHT & FAR RIGHT: pre-glam David Bowie jams at a party thrown by publicist and future nightclub impresario and DJ Rodney Bingenheimer at lawyer Paul Figen's house in January 1971

A SPACE ODDITY

BOWIE STARCHILD

fancy free in the States where he took full advantage of his freedom, doing as much to promote himself as he could — wearing a Mr. Fish dress, for example, which gave him a disturbingly female look enhanced by wavy hair flowing over his shoulders. His apparent naiveté and helplessness disarmed and charmed everyone, and his English accent did the rest. He played the centre of attention to perfection. Soaking up the influences of musicians who were unafraid to stand on the edge, like Iggy pop, David returned to England invigorated by the new sights and sounds he had experienced, and his own creativity flared. His direction seemed clear to him now.

One of the songs he wrote at that time was called 'Oh! You Pretty Things' and one of the people impressed with the song was producer Mickie Most. The song went to number 12 in the charts, albeit sung by Peter Noone. While Bowie worked on a new image for himself, ridding the press releases of his post-hippie shackles, Noone praised the songwriter, and suddenly, David Bowie was the flavour of the month. Tony Defries was back in action, too; using Laurence Myers' money, he was determined to cut the record companies out of the action and give to David control of his own works.

Bathed in happy creative achievement, David was in a positive frame of mind, and his optimism was compounded by the birth of Duncan Zowie Haywood Bowie on May 30th. David wrote a song to celebrate the occasion; 'Kooks', heavily influenced by Neil Young. Outwardly everything appeared well with Angie, but the birth had been extremely difficult; in fact, she was suffering from postnatal depression, and left for Italy to recuperate with a friend. David didn't seem to notice.

Another band came to support Bowie for a concert at the BBC in June. Mick Ronson was back, as was 'Woody' together with Trevor Bolder on bass. As so often with David, preparations were last minute, yet the professionalism of the musicians coupled with David's performance and his Mr. Fish dress won the day. His whirling mind was now concentrated intensely on his career and he announced a new album; it was going to be called Hunky Dory.

Hunky-dory with its highlights 'Oh, You Pretty Things', 'Changes' and 'Life on Mars?' was built around the piano, and Bowie used Mick Ronson as an arranger as well as guitarist, a role which turned the guitarist into a bag of nerves with an impatient Bowie either

RIGHT: Being interviewed at his flat at Haddon Hall, Beckenham, London, 24th April 1972

A SPACE ODDITY

BOWIE STARCHILD

30

shouting at him or encouraging him. Bowie himself was almost perfect every take. This was the 'tasteful thief' at work picking the best creations from the best musicians and songwriters to produce colourful lyricism and cascading musical ideas. Behind the scenes, Defries used ruthless brinkmanship to free himself and Bowie of Mercury whilst being drawn into the singer's world and he was intent on getting American record label RCA interested in David. To achieve that result, he and David made a trip to America in September 1971.

David continued his charm offensive, which he had now honed to a fine art in itself, and in Richard Robinson, RCA's house producer and his music journalist wife Lisa, David had powerful new admirers on his side. Defries sealed the deal on the 9th of September making the Bowie camp $37,500 better off, and after so many setbacks, David was on his way to stardom.

It was during this exciting visit to America that he met the likes of Andy Warhol and Lou Reed and he had a meeting with someone who would prove crucial to the glamorous image David would project on stage; Iggy pop. Iggy was almost like David's alter ego, his outrageous lifestyle even more far-fetched than anything David could have imagined; understandably, David became obsessed with him.

Back in England, at a gig on the 25th of September, David tried out a costume of red platform boots, baggy black culottes and a woman's beige jacket that revealed his naked chest. The obvious success made him ecstatic, and he became impatient to get another album started.

ZIGGY STARDUST WAS ABOUT TO RISE TO GLORY.

LEFT: Being interviewed at his flat at Haddon Hall, Beckenham, London, 24th April 1972

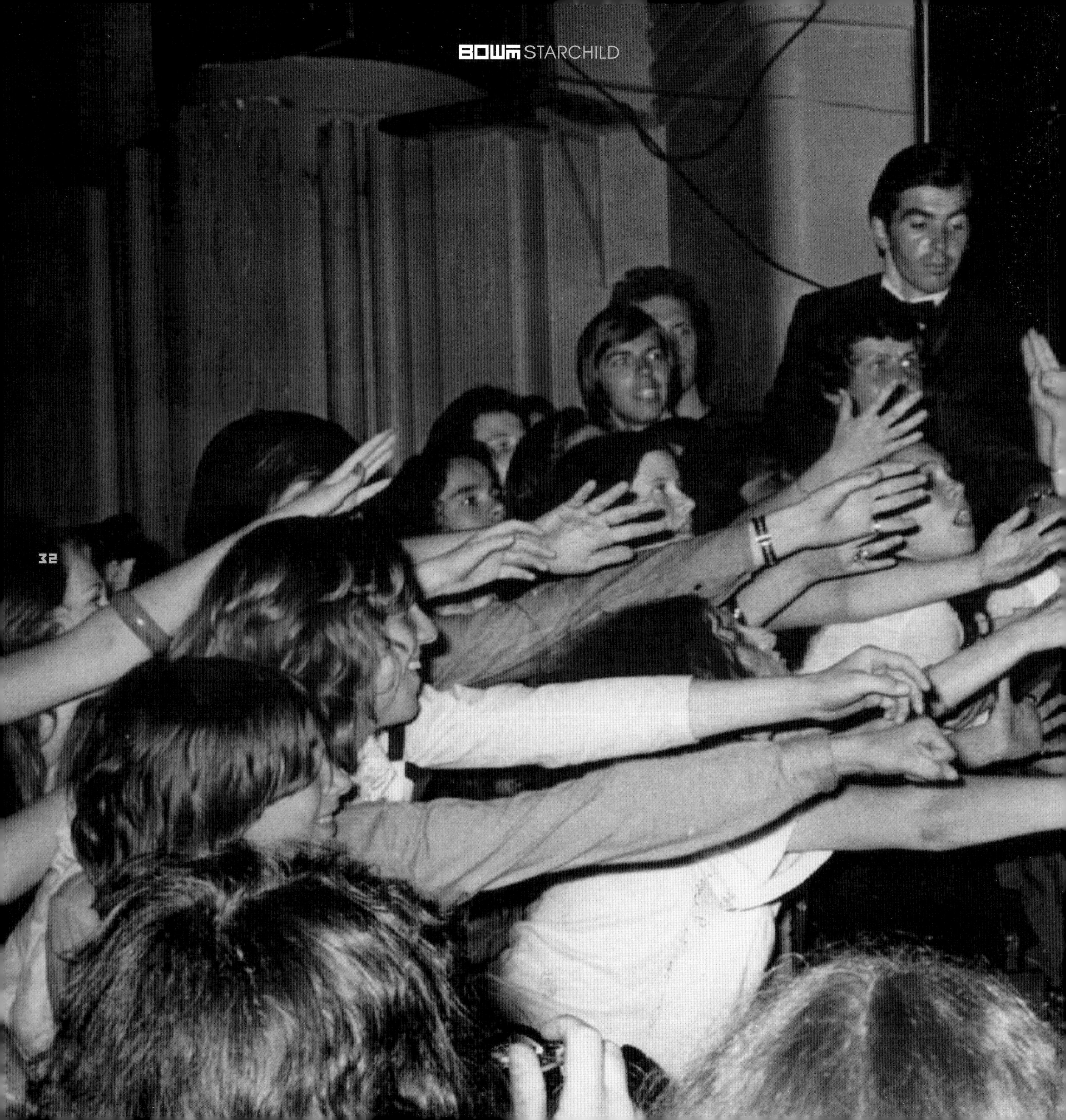

ABOVE: Concert at the Hammersmith Odeon, on 3rd July 1973, the last concert performed in the guise of his spacerocker character Ziggy Stardust

BOWIE STARCHILD

34

ABOVE & RIGHT: Performing onstage during his 'Ziggy Stardust' era, 1973

A SPACE ODDITY

STARCHILD

ABOVE: Mick Ronson performing with Ziggy Stardust and The Spiders From Mars at the Hammersmith Odeon, 1973

LEFT: Ziggy Stardust And The Spiders From Mars pose for a portrait in November 1972

A SPACE ODDITY

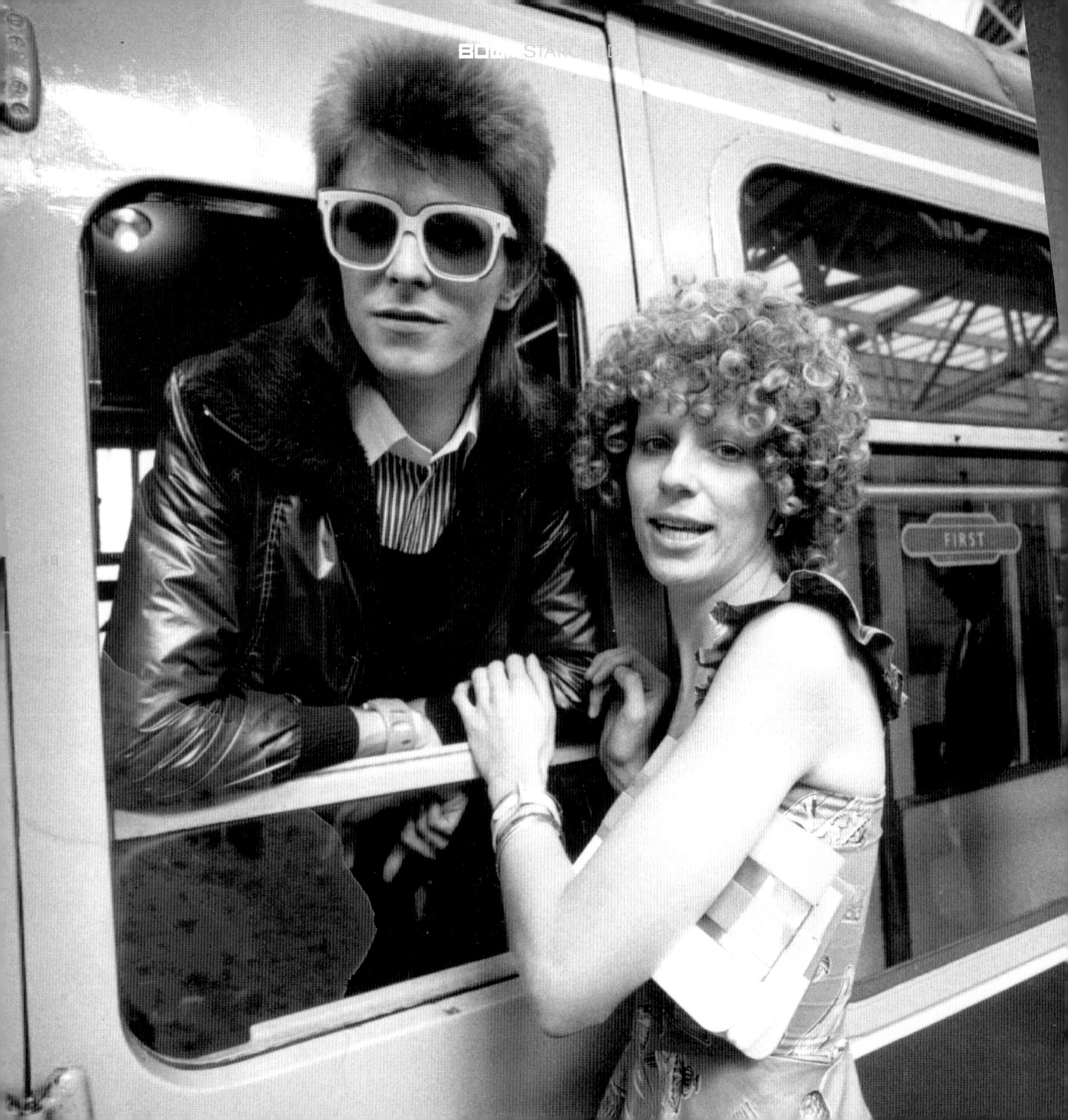
FIRST

ABOVE: 'Ziggy Stardust' era in August 1973

LEFT: Bowie is seen off at the station by his wife Angie

A SPACE ODDITY

BOWIE STARCHILD

Although David maintained that Ziggy came to him in a dream, he owed his birth to the scorched star Iggy Pop, behind whose glittering facade was the puppet master Jim Osterberg, who could execute and excuse his excesses through Iggy. Ziggy was the glamorous champion of the outsider, just as Bowie saw himself, and the album went though the register of sleazy undertones; rocker, rebel, champion of sexual liberation, fallen angel. Bowie bought wrestling boots and colourful material for Ziggy's skin-tight outfit, and Bowie's other angel, Angie, helped the final part of the look come about; the short hair.

David wanted to be the spokesperson for a new generation of philosophy and meaning-thirsty freedom seekers and was forming out of himself the product he was going sell to them. To that end, he announced to the musical press that he was gay, although for all his ability to slip into men's lustful thoughts as well as women's, the way he said it made his listeners doubt that the real David Bowie stood behind his words. Not so many years later he would retract the statement when he thought that it had damaged him in his biggest market, America, so the accusations about Bowie using sexual orientation as a marketing strategy seem justified. Later, this was admitted, albeit obliquely.

Yet, the ripples that this pop idol would cause by his glittering, enigmatic image were far more significant than his presumed deceit; they changed the world for a generation of youngsters.

The new dawn soon arrived, coupling Bowie's name with the word 'star' for the first time. And the single that Bowie almost dashed off just to dive into the market became a legend; it was 'Starman'.

Just before the release of Ziggy, Bowie had written a song for Mott the Hoople; 'All the Young Dudes', was Bowie's vivid depiction of lost youth, his homage to rock 'n' roll, his real love. Had he decided to sing it himself it might have changed his career entirely with swift and enormous success.

The excitement in the air surrounding him was palpable, everybody felt that this time Bowie was going to take off.

The Rise and Fall of Ziggy Stardust and the Spiders From Mars – the Spiders From Mars being the back up band – hit the streets on June the 6th, 1972. In their reviews, writers homed in on the perennial accusation; the work was a mishmash compilation of the styles and sounds of a myriad of other musicians.

As Starman began its rise upwards in the charts, David was refining his Ziggy outfits, in other words, making them more flamboyant still. And once more it was Angie who egged him on to evermore improbable experiments. And as his star status rose, those around him began to notice the subtle change that was taking place in the singer; he seemed to be gradually retreating from those around him into the world inhabited by the idol his fans adored. He believed that he was special, and as so many have done before and since, he fell for his own hype. He could keep audiences of thousands wrapped in his spell; his concerts were rampant successes. David was where he had always wanted to be.

It was next stop America, which David and Angie reached on September the 17th for a tour of venues that for all the hype generated by the slick Defries were often yawningly empty. This worried Bowie. Days of intense activity would slide into days of slothfulness, creative ideas would be left unborn due to the demands of touring. It all served to unbalance many who of those were on the tour. Still, David was ecstatic to be travelling through the country that had been the stuff of fantasies for him. And the rolling bus produced 'Jean Genie', although assistance at its birth was claimed by some of the others on the tour. The song eventually peaked at

RIGHT: Bowie performs live on stage at Earls Court Arena on May 12 1973 during the Ziggy Stardust tour

41

A SPACE ODDITY

ABOVE & RIGHT: Performing 'Rebel Rebel' on the TV show TopPop on 7th February 1974 in Hilversum, Netherlands

A SPACE ODDITY

44

ABOVE: Angie Bowie, Zowie Bowie (Duncan Jones) and David Bowie appear at a press conference at the Amstel Hotel on 7th February 1974 in Amsterdam

BOWIE STARCHILD

number 2 in the UK following its release in November.

And in Los Angeles there awaited a life of hedonism, sex with groupies and drugs on tap, a dangerous place to be for a man slipping into an alternate reality. Scientology did the rounds in the band to further intoxicate the mix, and Angie did her bit by having affairs, one of which was with James Williamson, the guitarist of Iggy Pop's band the Stooges', who were also touring under Tony Defries' management MainMain. To aggravate matters, Williamson bore no love for David.

So, Bowie loved America, but what did America think of Bowie? On October 14th 1972, the New Yorker came out with an article that read, *"What Bowie offers is not 'decadence' (sorry, Middle America) but a highly professional pop surface with a soft core: under that multi-coloured day-glow frogman's outfit lurks the soul of a folkie who digs Brel, plays an (amplified) acoustic guitar, and sings with a catch in his voice about the downfall of the planet."*

But despite it all, the shows that took place on October the 20th and 21st in Los Angeles were glittering successes. Yet the tour remained somewhat fractured, with semi-empty auditoria and British–American conflicts breaking out amongst the entourage. And the convenience that was their *"open marriage"*, a calling card that David was happy to use to prove his credentials as a subversive, was starting to crack under the strain. David's public affairs had got under Angie's skin and now it seemed her affairs had taken on the nature of revenge acts; she took a semi-permanent lover, much in the way that a Frenchman might take a mistress, by the name of Scott Richardson, a friend of Iggy's. As the rift deepened, friends' loyalties were stretched; the situation became ugly, and Defries, who disliked Angie's loud, driven character anyway, set about uncoupling her from the touring crew. No wives allowed on the road was the new rule, and David, despite his dependence on Angie, bowed to Defries' will.

Back in England, the Bowie family spent

RIGHT: A portrait of David Bowie, 1974

Christmas together whilst Bowie began work on a new album, Aladdin Sane, which was hurried through the recording studio, although intermittently interrupted by live gigs. Then it was back to America for a second tour in February 1973.

The problems that arose on that tour would lead to a parting of the ways between Ziggy and the Spiders. Suddenly made aware that the other band members were being hugely underpaid in comparison to the new pianist, Mick Ronson set about making a separate deal with CBS. Defries soon found out, however, and informed David whilst apparently calming the situation with counteroffers, such as a Ronson solo album deal. But the damage had been done.

Before matters came to a head, a new exciting venture had been planned; a tour of Japan, where the Bowie circus landed on the 5th of April 1973. Japanese youngsters lapped up this theatrical explosion, hordes of them assaulted the stage doors after the shows and Bowie enjoyed the strangeness of Japanese culture.

The touring continued back in the UK, Bowie high in the clouds as the press trumpeted that here was an inspired talent, and he and the band burst like exotic fireworks into the grey towns of a strike-ridden Britain.

But all was not well in paradise. The constant touring and the monotony meant that the concerts were becoming tiresome rather than fun, and relationships suffered under the strain of constant contact on and off the stage. The band felt that they were being squeezed to death, and the effect on David was both physically and mentally detrimental. He had become pale and tense, haggard, even, and began to seem physically frail; he had lost his enthusiasm for all that Ziggy

BOWIE STARCHILD

embodied and felt simply *"... wasted and miserable"*. This push to make profits while the sun was shining was not working in the way Defries had hoped, and the pyramid that he had built, MainMain, was looking decidedly shaky financially. Worse, the exhausting touring schedule had left David empty of further inspiration.

To stave off the collapse of his star, Defries decided that the singer should stop performing for a while and jettison Ziggy, which would avoid the public collapse of his star's momentum — and Defries' company. Who decided what is a moot point – although Bowie was now reliant on his manager for all decisions and deferred to him in all things almost meekly – so during the last show in the UK promoting the Aladdin Sane album at the Hammersmith Odeon in London on July 3rd 1973, the 60th gig in the UK, Bowie announced that not only was the concert *"... the last show of the tour, but it's the last show that we'll ever do."* Which came as bit of a shock to everyone as only Bowie, Defries, Ronson and Scott Richardson knew what was going on. The announcement coming as it did was pure Bowie, pure theatricality — and hurtful.

The next project was easy; an album called Pin Ups containing cover versions of his songs. With Angie playing less of a role in his life, he now had a live in/out lover much as Angie did; her name was Ava Cherry, and she would also provide background vocals for Bowie's songs. She also, briefly, moved into his and Angie's London home. By all accounts, Angie wasn't terribly happy with the arrangement. The album, however, was an instant success and entered the charts at number 1, even though reviews were scathing about the singer's over-indulgent vocals.

Before long, Mick Ronson, too, would part company with Bowie and launch his own successful solo career. His 1974 album Slaughter on 10th Avenue, would climb to number 9 in the UK charts.

Now cut adrift, David had moved with Angie and Zowie from Haddon Hall to fashionable Chelsea, where Ava stayed for a short while before moving into an apartment close by, and filled his days with creative projects, musical and personal. Whilst wading through books, he came to adopt the William Burroughs cutup technique for his own songs, splitting the lyrics and rearranging them into seemingly senseless snippets, some of them taken from the more quirky fan letters that he had received.

RIGHT: Bowie and Mick Ronson during their 'Ziggy Stardust & The Spiders From Mars' proof sheet from 1973

FAR RIGHT: Twiggy & Bowie in Paris for the cover of 'Pin Ups', 1973

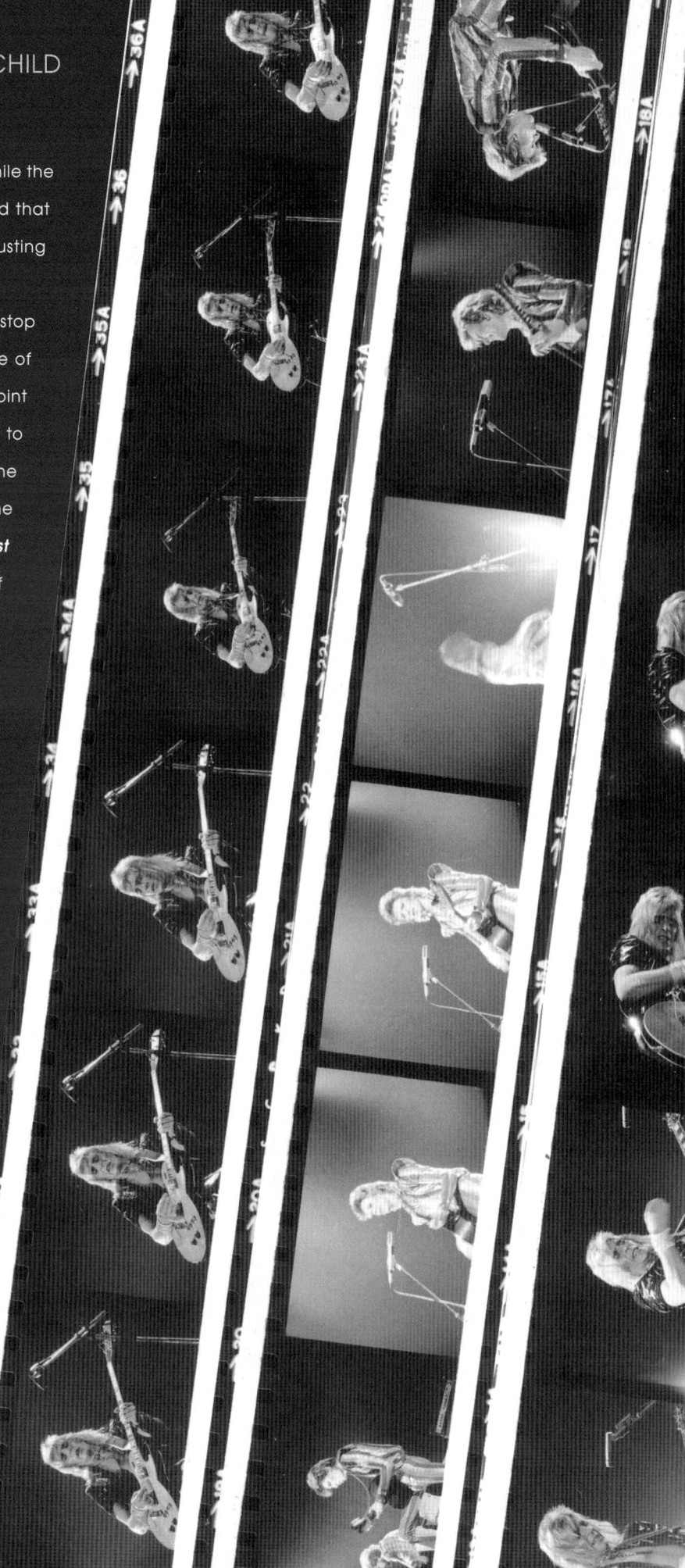

A SPACE ODDITY

BOWIE STARCHILD

Bathing in the sunshine of adoration and success, David should have been confidently riding the crest of the wave. But with Bowie, things were not as they first appeared to be, and his dependence on Defries to orchestrate his life was almost as absolute as the dependence on the drugs that would almost kill him. The realisation of this, according to Ava Cherry, would cause the singer to derail himself. Now, with Defries absent, living in the US and concentrating his business affairs there, red lights were flashing in Bowie's life.

Although he saw himself as a new version of the human male, Bowie displayed disturbingly unhealthy, conventional human tendencies such as fixating on things and people, being swayed by bright new discoveries, being rather unfocused and jealous of the greats of rock music such as Mick Jagger. In fact, Mick Jagger became another obsession to the extent that when another album began to form in Bowie's head, the Stones provided Bowie's musical map. Diamond Dogs was Bowie jettisoning Ziggy in favour of the Rolling Stones, and with Alan Parker and bassist Herbie Flowers on board he was in good hands. It was a break with a past world of lightness, too.

For the world he inhabited was disintegrating as he recorded; MainMain was imploding with the weight of profligate spending, so he found it hard to get hold of money he was owed; and he had no **"mates"** behind him when he sang. There was no mentor on hand to guide him. Soon, he got himself into an argument and was barred from the studio where he was recording. Inevitably, David's oppressed mental condition influenced the Diamond Dogs album, taking it along dark paths so that the music was imbued with foreboding and the lyrics followed suit.

There was help on hand, however; cocaine. The drug that helped Iggy to a mental institution. It told the user that they were free to behave as they wished; fatal for someone of Bowie self-absorbed inclinations, a man who could cold-shoulder anyone who had incurred his displeasure, even old friends.

Ava remembers the Bowie of that period as being angry, and initially, he took it to calm himself down. It was the start of a trip to hell and, to Bowie's credit, back.

It was around this time that another woman entered his life, Corinne 'Coco' Schwab, who had been hired to run the UK branch of MainMain and soon devoted herself entirely to David. She became all things to her needy child; lover, confidante, a sister figure, a second mother, and she was immortalised in one of David songs, 'Never Let Me Down'.

"Coco was the one person who told me what a fool I was becoming and she made me snap out of it."

With the intention of moving to America permanently, David landed in New York in April 1974, by which time he was already enslaved to cocaine, trembling hands included. It was the same month that Diamond Dogs was released to mixed reviews.

But there was a new show to plan to promote the album, and keep him from self-destructing entirely.

The set for the tour was designed as a futuristic 'Hunger City', with cherry pickers, movable bridges and catwalks, a glass 'asylum' and a boxing ring; there were also some designs drawn from the work of German artist George Grosz. As for the Bowie image, that changed too; the carrot top vanished, his hair was now parted with a floppy fringe as he copied Bryan Ferry's persona, adopting Ferry's double-breasted suits style and his stage movements.

The show opened in Canada, and the huge technical difficulties meant that every night was **"fun and dangerous"**, as David remembered, and equipment and hydraulics broke down. He admitted later that he was

RIGHT: **A colour-enhanced image of English singer and musician David Bowie, exaggerating his heterochromia iridis, 1973. This photo was taken in Paris during a photoshoot for Bowie's 'Pin Ups'**

51

A SPACE ODDITY

BOWIE STARCHILD

stoned for the length of the tour, which one of the musicians later described as *"pantomime"*. In fact, the people around him were worried about the awful physical appearance of this fragile singer. David dismissed their worries, for even as the pantomime wound its way through the States, he had already lost interest in it and was planning another radical change.

With forties clothes borrowed from Ava Cherry — they had belonged to her musician father — Bowie started work on a new album during a break from touring in the month of August. He was buzzing when he went to the studio to record the album Young Americans with Tony Visconti. David was obsessive about soul music and R&B and used New York guitarist Carlos Alomar and his wife, the singer Robin Clarke, as well as Luther Vandross to add authenticity to the sessions. Bowie and Alomar's working relationship would span 30 years.

David was in his element, free to work in the way that he loved; the musicians would lay down the tracks first and David would marshal his ideas, write basic lyrics and then go home to write before returning to finish off the session with his vocals. The title track for the new album was recorded the very first day, and the change in style from what had gone before was dramatic. The lyrics were reflections, slices of life, the musical accompaniment funky, and his voice, too, had morphed into a Bryan Ferry/big band era croon.

THE RESULTS WERE STARTLING.

Writer Paul Trynker describes one track on the album, **'It's Gonna Be Me'**, as one of the most *"accomplished vocal performances"* that David Bowie had ever recorded. Although there were critics aplenty of Bowie's version of soul, Bowie had not tried to pretend that he was either a soul singer or a torchbearer for that tradition. For him, the genre was another means of expressing what couldn't be expressed as dramatically in any other way.

Once he had immersed himself in his new persona, he wanted nothing to do with the overly flamboyant

LEFT: 1974 Diamond Dogs tour on stage in Los Angeles

tour he had been dragging around behind him since June. When the tour resumed in October, it was no longer the 'Diamond Dogs Tour', because Bowie had renamed it the 'Soul Tour'.

So the new reshaped tour continued on its way, fuelled, it seems, by the bags of cocaine that lay around everywhere. And everyone on stage revelled in their work. Yet the drugs also made David insecure and he refused to go on stage without its help. Behind-the-scenes, meanwhile, his private life was being dismantled in a whirling pool of chaos; his sex life, divided between Coco, Ava and Angie, pitted the three women against each other. Angst-ridden, David would call up Angie only to ignore her when she arrived to see him; and he discovered that he had made friends with the idea of ending their relationship.

There was an even more devastating discovery in store for Bowie, however.

He had been under the mistaken impression that he owned half of the MainMain company along with Tony Defries. When it was made clear to him that this was absolutely not the case, his world and his belief in Tony Defries, crashed down brutally onto the coke-filled singer. The news paralysed him, and instead of trying to clarify the situation, all he wanted to do was banish Tony and everything to do with him, from his life. Confronted with his own childish naïveté and self-deception and the damage they had done to him, his self-esteem took an almost knockout blow. He was overtaken by uncontrollable fits of crying. Luckily, either Ava or Coco would be there to comfort and ease his agony.

In the midst of all this, David arrived in Hollywood for his concerts there and was surrounded by showbiz glamour; Elton John and Elizabeth Taylor to mention but two. But the signs of strain were already showing with David as likely as not to turn up dishevelled and behave oddly. He became increasingly isolated and lonely as the factions around him jealously danced around one another off stage; yet onstage, at sound checks or whenever he was involved in playing music, David was alive, focused

RIGHT: Bowie posing with a large barking dog while working on the artwork for his 1974 album 'Diamond Dogs'

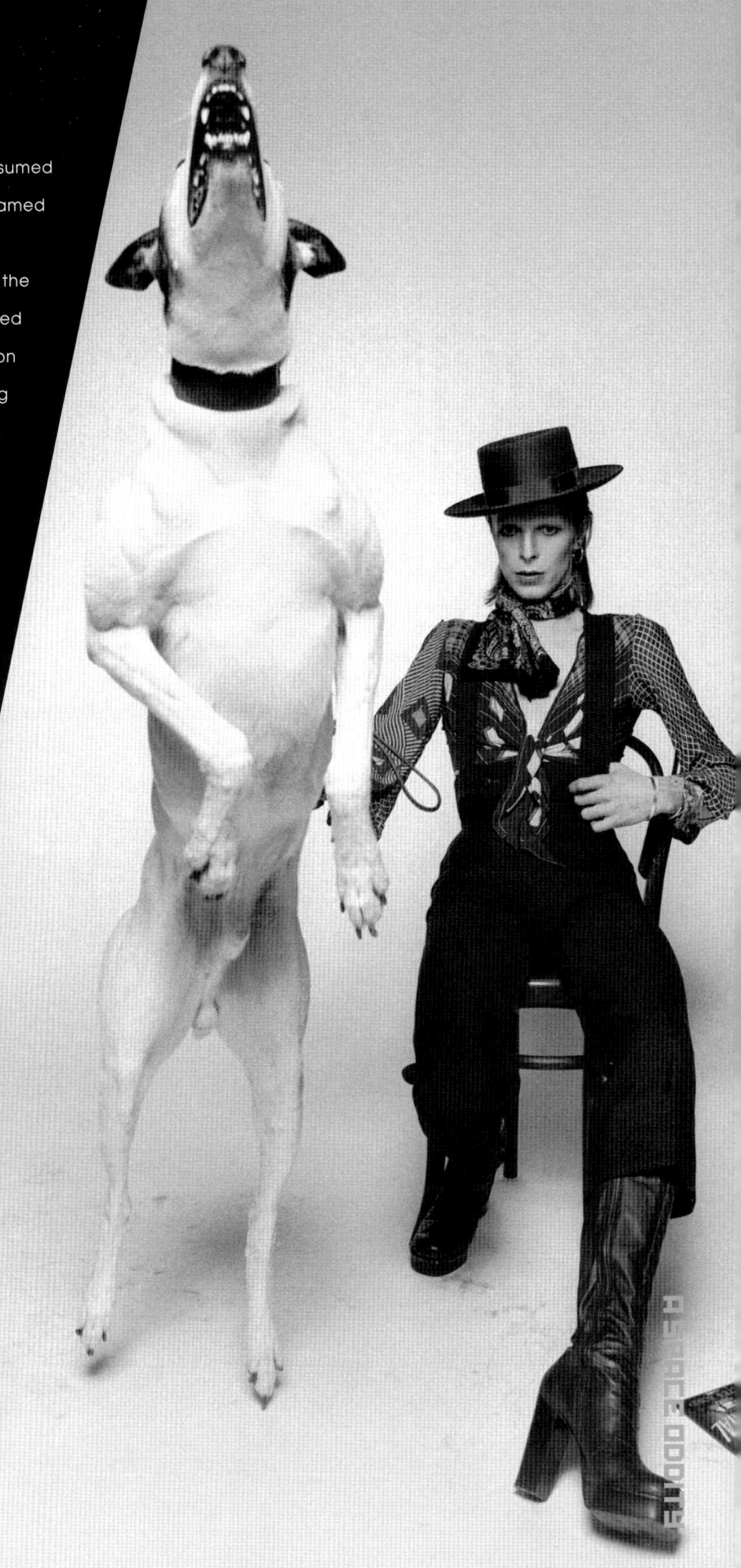

and energised, as he was whenever Zowie was around.

David's Dick Cavett Show appearance during the tour is now famous for Bowie's druggie interview with his host, as he fumbles around with his cane, unable to remain still for a moment and sniffing constantly. But he was aware enough to speak coherently and tried to deflect criticism by being modest and coy. In a generally long-drawn out interview, one of his moments of truth came when he said that he was a storyteller who acted out his stories although at that moment he was performing as himself; a fact of which Cavett was painfully aware.

In New York, David spent time with John Lennon and Paul McCartney, who also noticed Bowie's odd behaviour and need for approval and were surprised to see how far Bowie had descended into his coke habit. Nonetheless, John joined in work at the studio with David, and John's doodling on the guitar inspired Bowie to write what would become his biggest hit to date, 'Fame'. Set to music that is repetitive and mocking, the lyrics were rattled off in twenty minutes and built around the word fame that 'takes you there where things are hollow'; the song was sung from David's heart as he felt that he was now living in that hollow place. Fame found its way onto the Young Americans album and gave Bowie his first no 1 hit in the US. At least there was music to make life worthwhile whilst his life outside of it was in frightening disarray, if not decay. And whilst the coke revved up his creativity, it demanded a heavy toll from anyone walking along its paths.

That Christmas, David, floating in a coke cloud had finally lost patience with Defries, who was sinking money earned by David into grand projects that went down with all hands on deck — and David's money. David talked to Lennon, who had gone through similar problems, and felt vindicated in his decision to be free of Defries. Defries, for all his faults, had taken Bowie to where he wanted to be, albeit using a lot of his star's money to do so. But there was no violent breakup; they met and achieved little, it seems; but the two gradually slid apart, and as they did so, Defries' MainMain, his crazy emporium that spun and showered magic dust over everyone, especially David, deflated behind them. The merry go round was slowly coming to a halt.

The breakup brought disagreement over rights, of course, and problems that snaked into David's future as he came to understand that what he had created had not belonged to him from the moment the ideas left his head. The tapes masters belonged to Defries. Once Bowie had finally got to grips with this notion, that he was not truly free, his anger at his imprisonment was only ever lurking behind the next word.

David's fragile physical and mental state at the time was uniquely captured in a music documentary made in 1974 by Alan Yentob of the BBC during the Diamond Dogs tour. Appropriately called 'Cracked Actor', it showed excerpts from the Ziggy Stardust film and from the Hammersmith Odeon concert of 3rd July 1973 and followed the star into hotels and limousines. David appears, indeed, hollow and alone, ill, a victim of his own spider web. When he saw the film later, Bowie remarked that he was *"... so stoned... when I see that now I cannot believe I survived it. I was so close to really throwing myself away physically, completely"*.

And he wasn't too great mentally either, looking at the interview he gave to Creem Magazine at the time. *"Dictatorship"* was the answer to the ills besetting society declared Bowie. *"You've got to have an extreme right front come up and sweep everything off its feet and tidy everything up. Then you can get a new form of liberalism.... so the best thing that can happen is for an extreme right Government to come. It'll do something positive, at least, to cause commotion in people and they'll either accept the dictatorship or get rid of it... my predictions are very accurate ... always."*

David has never displayed fascist leanings, but he was never just interested, he was always obsessed, and he would watch movies about Nazis, endlessly.

RIGHT: Bowie on stage at the Universal Amphitheatre, Los Angeles in October 1974 during his Diamond Dogs tour

A SPACE ODDITY

55

BOWIE STARCHILD

56

ABOVE: Bowie on stage at the Universal Amphitheatre, Los Angeles in October 1974 during his Diamond Dogs tour

A SPACE ODDITY

BOWIE STARCHILD

That, paired with his reports about UFO sightings, meant that David's thoughts were alarming to others.

Just as it seemed that David was losing control completely, another woman stepped in to distract him, at least temporarily, from destruction. Her name was Maggie Abbott a theatrical agent, who found in David Bowie the perfect man for a lead role in a film being prepared, called The Man Who Fell to Earth. The alien, druggie disconnect, the strangely light, factitious voice, was exactly the quality the film company was looking for, even though, at first sight, Bowie made an eerie impression; stick thin and with grey teeth. Hardly surprising, as he was said to be living on a cocaine and milk diet. And then, after an almost violent confrontation with Jimmy Page, the Led Zeppelin guitarist, Bowie went speeding towards the works of Aleister Crowley, an occultist known as **"The wickedest man in the world"**. Page had been interested in Crowley's works for many, many years before Bowie became interested. This was a new and dangerous turn in the Bowie story. There were reports of him drawing pentagrams on the wall, chanting spells, and investigating the devil's power, and comparing it all to the Jewish mystical system of the Kabbalah.

It seemed that the music world of New York was turning against him, now, and a move to Los Angeles for a film seemed to offer the perfect way out. His new manager, Michael Lippman, who said that his client **"... can be very charming and friendly, and at the same time he can be very cold and self-centred"** and was saying he **"wanted to rule the world"**, lived there, too. Bowie would not, however, escape his increasing dependency on cocaine. The bass player for the band Deep Purple, Glenn Hughes, befriended Bowie in LA and with him indulged in what was a frightening addiction to cocaine that produced what Glenn described as **"a dark year"**, which Bowie was reluctant to speak about in later years. It was a good friendship for Bowie that brought laughter; but ultimately he was still isolated and lost.

David caught a glimpse of the future when he met Iggy Pop again in LA. Iggy had ended up a drooling, psychiatric heap of crumbled humanity thanks to his drug habit and was in a terrible physical condition. David simply offered him more drugs. Bowie himself was sliding into mental delusion and hanging out with other addicts, and his mind would race even more than it ever had, with his drug of choice.

When Ava visited, she was afraid of this man, now alien to her, who continuously spoke about ghosts in the present and past. Their relationship was soon nothing but a ghost of the past. Apart from occasional visitors, David, in the weeks before filming started, was more alone with his paranoia than ever.

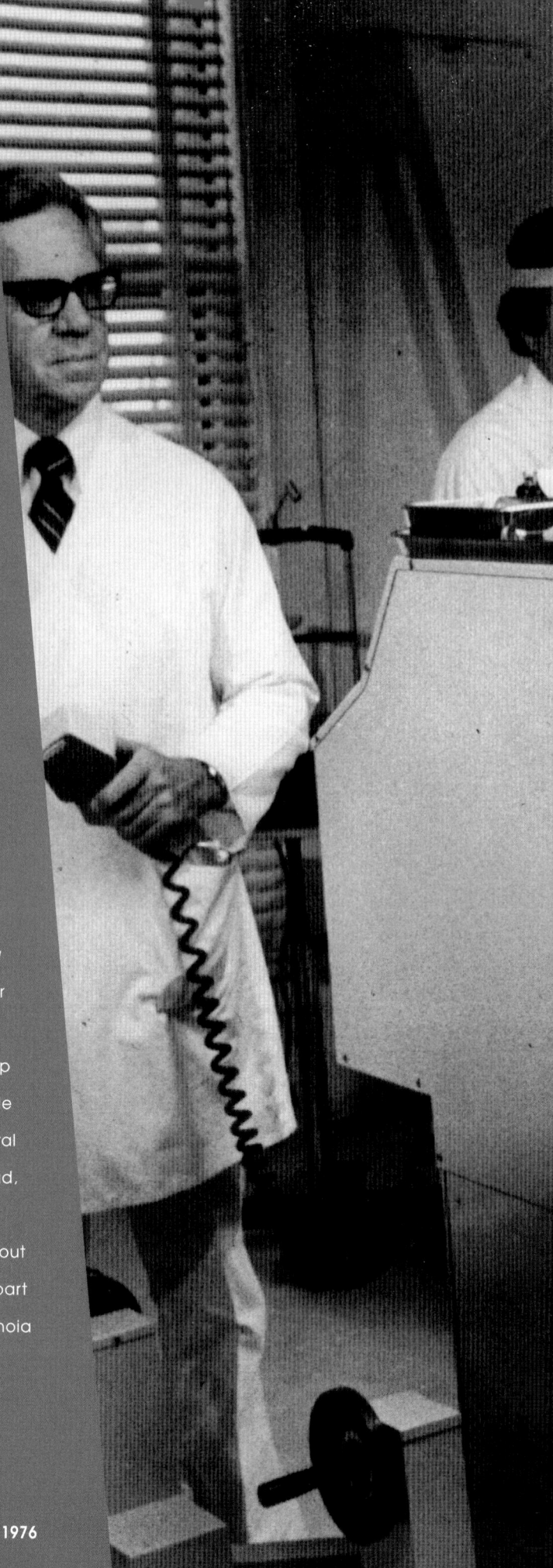

RIGHT: Scientists experiment on David Bowie in a scene from the film 'The Man Who Fell To Earth', 1976

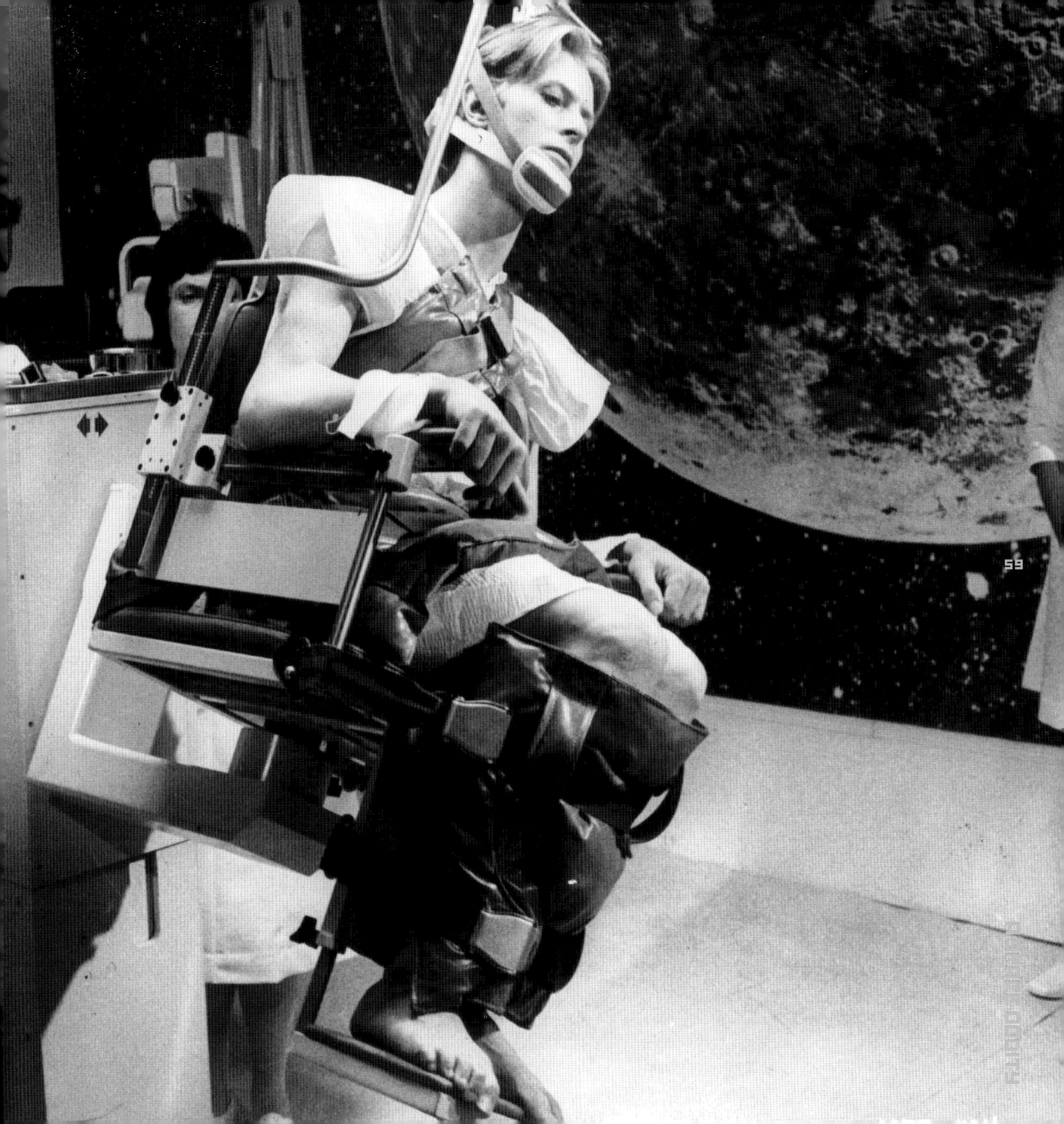

BOWM STARCHILD

INSET: 'The Man Who Fell To Earth' poster

MAIN IMAGE: David Bowie in a scene from the film 'The Man Who Fell To Earth', 1976

A SPACE ODDITY

BOWIE STARCHILD

SAVED IN BERLIN

"I play the starring role. How about that for a piece. Isn't he a jammy bugger that Bowie. I don't know… in the business five minutes and he's taking work away from veterans!"

These words were spoken during the Creem interview in February 1975, with Bowie, it seems, gloatingly defensive; but although it didn't seem like it at the time, the work on the film marked a subtle turning point in his life.

Director Nicholas Roeg decided not to intervene should David indulge his drug habit during filming. Bowie's mental state was perfect for the role and rather than unbalance his star altogether, he decided to just let things run and see what happened. Bowie commented later that what was needed for the for the role was, **"Just being me, as I was perfectly adequate for the role. I wasn't of this earth at that particular time."**

One of his co-stars described him as, **"… really at the height of his beauty. He had really thick hair that he dyed that lovely colour and his skin was just gorgeous."**

"He was very removed and quiet", said his co-star Candy Clark, **"… clear as a bell, focused, friendly and professional".**

He got through the filming, and **"The Man Who Fell To Earth"** remains the greatest acting achievement of his career. His performance was praised as being **"… incomparable, one of a kind"**, and many critics felt the same way.

For David, it seemed as though this film might be his breakthrough into the movie industry, his entree into the first rank of media stars.

He eagerly began planning another album. Surrounded by waves of coke-saturated ideas, he wanted to simply walk into a studio and record. Experimentation was the keyword, a trip in more ways than one, into an auditory Grand Canyon. Bowie's musicians often had no idea what their musical contributions were for, but as in previous recording sessions, the band was as much part of the creative process as the singer was, filling in, extending and ornamenting Bowie's musical ideas. Yet David was always in control whatever his own state of mind, completely logical and focused on the music. And this, despite the tales that the curtains of his home were permanently drawn, that black candles would burn whilst he sat on the floor scrawling pentagrams. He weighed less than seven stone at one stage, and ate nothing but red and green peppers and milk, which he consumed in the early hours of the morning. High on coke and buzzing with energy, he'd stay awake for seven or eight days in a row, hallucinating and inhabiting doom-laden visions. According to Angie, he had his

RIGHT: Bowie poses for a portrait in 1976

63

SAVED IN BERLIN

pool, in which the devil appeared, exorcised. Unsurprisingly, Station to Station includes inevitable references to Crowley and the occult, but at the same time nods to Christianity because, as Bowie later admitted, the title referred to the stations of the cross.

In 1997, Bowie opened up about his state of mind at the time: **"I was just paranoid, manic depressive... the usual paraphernalia that comes with the abuse of amphetamines and coke"**, and said he could remember nothing about making the album.

Station to Station was Bowie the creative improviser, bravely covering new musical territory, pushing himself to discover what was inside his head without a structure to fall back on, foregoing reliance on what had gone before, what was comfortingly familiar. He was, once again, pushing away all that he had achieved in order to explore what was new and exciting. The co-producer on Young Americans, Harry Maslin, returned to record Station to Station and he recalls that David had no specific sound or direction in mind for the album, he was simply intent on recording a commercial album. He changed his mind so completely and so often, Maslin commented, that **"... It's hard to tell at times what he's talking about"**. As the lyrics were riddled with the influences of his occult searches, that is hardly surprising. Guitarist Earl Slick adds that David did have a song or two written, but by the time they were recorded they no longer resembled the original songs.

Station to Station was released in January 1976, and Bowie's courage in forging ahead and attempting to find a new musical language was understood by the musical press and rewarded by his fans with a number 3 spot in the charts. For some people, the album was his pièce de résistance, the culmination of everything that had gone before; the summit which no other album could climb. Even years later, writers felt that he had never looked or sounded better, his enigmatic texts adding to his glamour with a remarkable backing band moving between the funk and soul sounds of Young Americans and the electronic sparking that would come in Berlin.

1976 had seen The Thin White Duke bubble to the surface of David Bowie's cocaine ocean. This Bowie incarnation wore a white shirt, a waistcoat and black trousers, a stylish costume and the least flamboyant that Bowie had adopted to date. Yet the Duke has been described as **"an amoral zombie"**, a man singing songs of intense feeling, who felt nothing himself. David called this period **"the darkest days of my life"**, and it didn't take long for him to jettison the thin White

RIGHT: Bowie poses for a portrait in 1976

Duke, who he had come to regard as *"a nasty character indeed"*. And yet; *"What I'm doing is theatre, and only theatre... What you see on stage isn't sinister. It's pure clown. I'm using myself as a canvas and trying to paint the truth of our time on it."* Not even David, it seems, understood what he was up to. This character, erotically louche despite his apparent stylishness, was David Bowie's way of appealing to a more intellectual European audience.

The soundtrack to The Man Who Fell to Earth had also been placed in his hands and he began work in November with the arranger Paul Buckmaster. But writing the soundtrack to a film required a different mindset to producing songs that could go where they wished, and with Bowie still floating around on his own planet, the music, said Buckmaster, did not come up to scratch. Director Nicholas Roeg was looking for a more folksy sound, although composer John Phillips thought that Bowie's compositions were *"haunting and beautiful"*. The creative problems eventually led to some stock music being used, with Mick Taylor, former Rolling Stones guitarist, Stomu Yamash'ta, the Japanese percussionist and John Phillips, formerly with The Mamas and the Papas, brought in to take up the slack. Bowie blamed his manager for this humiliation and ejected him from his circle.

Iggy Pop, on the other hand, who had fallen about as low as it was possible to get, suddenly found himself back in and under David's wing, with David offering to help him make an album. During the Station to Station tour of 1976, David and Iggy's friendship deepened and these ostensibly similar, but in character very different personalities, would spend a lot of time together engrossed in the exploration of musical interests and personal agonies. And their renewed friendship led to both men agreeing to kick their drug habits. It was a sign that the hollow days were coming to an end for both of

BOWIE STARCHILD

them. David even managed to describe himself as *"at peace"* after a concert, a far cry from the days when he had been in the firm grip of fame mania.

It was during the tour in America that he met another man who influenced his life in a profound manner. The man was writer Christopher Isherwood, and a conversation with him planted a seed in the singer's mind; to live and record in Berlin, Germany.

The tour schedule brought David to Europe next, where his shows were a roaring success, and his meeting with the glamorous Berlin transgender nightclub owner Romy Haag sealed the deal for Bowie, confirming that the atmosphere in the German capital would be ideal for him. Rumour, at least, made Haag David's muse.

Controversy followed Bowie on the tour when he was accused of making a Nazi salute. When the fascism accusations blew up in the press, Bowie was quick to deny them, and the salute was certainly a non-event. But there was left a sneaking suspicion that David would say anything to protect his career from his own off-the-cuff remarks.

The Station to Station tour ended in France on the 18th of May, and the post-concert party brought David and Romy together again.

And it was in France that David hired a studio in the Château d'Hérouville in the Val d'Oise département of France near Paris, where he would concentrate all his energies on a new album for Iggy Pop. The recordings began in July after Bowie had stopped off in Switzerland, briefly, where Angie was trying to entice him back into the nest, and Berlin, where he was, perhaps, searching for an apartment.

The album The Idiot was a genuine collaboration between the newly reunited friends, and most commentators consider that while David composed the music, Iggy was responsible for the lyrics, although the two inevitably changed roles. The *"Dum Dum Boys"* was Iggy's music, for example.

Cosy harmonies descended around David's life as he explored new strains in music that took him down exciting paths, while Coco Schwab provided him with physical warmth and took care of irritating small details in his life and work environments. Those details are a little hard to come by, and either David was still a cokehead in the grip of paranoia who would abandon a recording session, or he was simply a beer-drinking womaniser, depending on which tales you prefer. The sessions moved to Munich, where the two musicians continued their experimentation, obviously getting great enjoyment out of their musical project and each other's company, even though outsiders found them somewhat *"odd"*.

Towards the end of the summer, David was in Berlin and Iggy had moved in with him as they put the finishing touches to Iggy's album with the help of Tony Visconti.

The three went out together as David explored his new city, a city that seemed to reflect his personality, a schizophrenic city that floated between its fascist past, the decadent remnants of its Weimar past, and it's uncertain future as an island in a sea of hostile communism, occupied by Allied military and inhabited by rebellious youth. David revelled in every aspect of it from the gay clubs to the cafes, the museums to the bookshops with the old Third Reich publications. Hitler's Germany still held a fascination for him as, indeed, it did for many. David tore himself away from his new surroundings to begin work on an album back at the Château d'Hérouville in France in September.

Back in experimental mode, David seemed, to all intents and purposes, to be at ease and enjoying himself; apart from an incident where Angie turned up and sparks flew together with drinking glasses. There was a new face in the studio control room not long after the session started, in the form of Brian Eno, who David had known since the days of Ziggy Stardust. It was a fruitful coalition that would have far reaching effects on the album and it gave David someone with whom he could share the humour of which he was badly in need.

LEFT: Image used for the Low album cover

BOWM STARCHILD

69

SAVED IN BERLIN

BOWIE STARCHILD

ABOVE: Bowie performs onstage at Olympia Stadium during the 'Station To Station' World Tour on February 29, 1976

Iggy also turned out to be a lifeline for David, for when Bowie was at his lowest ebb following gruelling days with lawyers, Iggy would haul him out of his depressions with humour, until everyone in the studio was rolling in the aisles with tales of mayhem from the past.

The new album, **"Low"**, turned out to be the first of three that became known as the **"Berlin Trilogy"**, despite the fact that it was mixed in Berlin but recorded in France, for the most part. With side one dedicated to avant-garde song fragments, and the second side given over to electronic music, the album represented a seismic shift in David Bowie's musical style. Brian Eno took over a great deal of the direction and composition for the electronics when David was in court fighting against his former manager Michael Lippman. Eno was also crucial in providing David with psychological support and siding with David in his opinion that no matter what the record companies said, they would forge ahead with their experimentation. The discussions about the album's commercialism was settled when they decided that seven songs would placate the fans' desire to hear the singer's voice, and the second side would be dedicated to instrumentals. David's pain could be heard through the unusual soundscapes, even though he was gradually escaping the claws of cocaine.

And it was Tony Visconti who was responsible for a unique addition to Bowie's album; he brought along an Eventide Harmoniser, which produced a huge percussion sound.

In October, everyone moved to Berlin to finish the project.

Influenced by German bands such as Neu and Kraftwerk, Low was considered ahead of its time and praised for its originality and inventiveness. Nonetheless, the critics were divided in their opinions, enjoying parts of it disliking others. Neither did Tony Defries, Nic Roeg and the RCA executives think much of the recording. But David was unshaken in his firm belief in what he had created.

Berlin offered David Bowie and Iggy pop, the chance to break with the lives they had known; it offered the peace Bowie required to stamp down his demons. It was a city where the two pop stars could take the underground trains unmolested and eat in quirky cafes or visit museums and antique shops in peace.

Coco had the walls of his apartment in an Art Nouveau building painted white, and she made sure that he had ready supplies of blank canvases and tubes of oil paint. She would read the German philosopher Nietzsche and she was beside him in the Brücke Museum, where they would look at the works of the Expressionists, those whose ideas seemed to mesh with Bowie's own imagination and state of mind; Kirchner, Kollwitz and Heckel.

There were, of course, tales of the two men falling back into their old ways; of them cruising through the city searching for fun and indulging in drinking sessions, after which they would stagger into gutters and transvestite bars or go out clubbing. One night, David apparently rammed the car belonging to their drug dealer for five manic minutes whilst Iggy sat in the passenger seat.

But through it all, the pair were still making music, and gradually, David came to realise that he no longer needed a mouthpiece through which to speak; he needed no alter egos flamboyantly proclaiming his ideas and what he wished to be. Now he was gaining the confidence to present himself to the world as he really was. He decided that he would not tour to promote the Low album but would, instead, tour with the Iggy to help market his album The Idiot, which was released in March 1977.

They opened the tour in England, and the fans hardly recognised the guitar player seated at the edge of the stage. This was a sober Bowie, who could now be seen in a flat cap, a check shirt or suit. No longer distant, he would chat happily to those around him.

David hadn't anticipated the amount of drug use that would take place backstage on the Iggy Pop tour and that worried him, but he still agreed to do a second album for his friend once the tour ended in America in April.

During the recording of that album, David continued to show that he was evolving into a different person. The album was written, recorded and mixed in eight days, speedy even for Bowie. Iggy commented that he had to think fast or David would think before him, but Iggy's spontaneous lyrical inventiveness spurred David on to use the same method in his next album. But Bowie was there as producer for his friend, and although he did an extraordinary job on the album, he was at all times prepared to accede to any ideas that Iggy wished to develop. Lust for Life was definitely Iggy's album and rose to number 28 in the UK.

Inspired, David set to work on his own album immediately. It, too, was completed quickly with the musicians hard at work from 12 noon until 8 in the evening to produce an album with a solid driving rock mood. As usual, music could be changed at a whim, and old session mate Carlos Alomar would provide a never-ending supply of melodies to weave gently through each piece.

Heroes was put together almost entirely in the studio, none of the songs had their structure before rehearsals began, a far cry from the days when Bowie songs would be set before he stepped into a studio. 'Joe the Lion', for example, came to life in one hour in front of the microphone. The album also boasted the talents of Robert Fripp, the former King Crimson guitarist, also a composer and record producer. Fripp had, in fact, retired from music but relented when Bowie rang him up.

The title song, 'Heroes', was also captured on tape very swiftly, and it became perhaps, David Bowie's best-known song, even though as a single it only reached number 24 in the UK charts. Brian Eno remembered the sessions in Berlin; Bowie *"... gets into a very peculiar state when he's working. He doesn't eat. It used to strike me as very paradoxical that two comparatively well-known people would be staggering home at six in the morning, and he'd break a raw egg into his mouth and that was his food for the day, virtually."*

ABOVE: Bowie and Iggy Pop perform live in 1977, San Francisco, California

SAVED IN BERLIN

BOWIE STARCHILD

ABOVE: Bowie arriving at Cherokee Recording Studio Hollywood, 1976

SAVED IN BERLIN

BOWM STARCHILD

Heroes was Bowie continuing to explore ambient music, the themes dark, the instrumentals atmospheric, looking into a future that, as David commented, would never come to pass. The album was released later in 1977 and the reviews were positive. It was named album of the year in both the NME and Melody Maker and rose to number 3 in the UK charts.

But Bowie's life, it seemed, was destined never to remain on an even keel for long. Having matured, having dropped the disingenuous 'please like me I'm a quirky small child' routine and found his way back to a more stable reality, he now surrounded himself with an entourage that once again distanced him from those around him. The heavy handedness of those employed to keep the world away from him, caused aggravation and hurt during the preparations of the show in England with Marc Bolan, David's erstwhile friend and rival glam rocker. And for David, always playing in the playground of dark thoughts, there was a terrible shock in store when Bolan was killed in a car crash in September 1977.

For David, this tragedy marked the end of a year of extraordinary creativity that had produced four albums that would have a huge impact on the future path of popular music.

The New Year of 1978 did not begin auspiciously; David and Angie's marriage was all but suffering from rigor mortis, but she had one last outburst to deliver in January when she tried to kill herself with sleeping pills before smashing all the glasses she could lay her hands on and throwing herself down the stairs, an act of pique that broke her nose and landed her in hospital.

In Berlin, David tried to keep his life steady with the help of Coco, but he would often disappear for days at a time to dose up on girls and drugs. And there was also an exciting project to occupy his mind; a film to be directed by David Hemmings called Just a Gigolo. The bait that got David hooked into the film was his co-star, Marlene Dietrich. As it turned out, the two never met because Dietrich would film her short contribution in Paris. So the film, shot in Berlin and in which Bowie played a Prussian officer in the Great War, never got into its stride. The film was so poorly received that it was withdrawn from the cinemas. So David was more than happy after this failure to plan his biggest tour ever, which would be known as the Isolar II – The 1978 World Tour.

LEFT: Berlin 1977: Robert Fripp, Brian Eno and Bowie while recording 'Heroes'

RIGHT: Bowie performs on stage at Earls Court Arena on August 28th, 1978

Carlos Alomar assumed the role of bandleader to the seven musicians. He was also invaluable in keeping the disparate characters on tour working together, acting as an unofficial psychologist to soothe troubled spirits. The set consisted of material from the albums Low and Heroes and included song sequences from The Rise and Fall of Ziggy Stardust and the Spiders from Mars. The concert closed with a selection from Station to Station. On stage, Bowie swathed himself in voluminous white baggy pants and a snakeskin drape coat in a set that consisted of a cage of tube lighting. The tour started in America and took up most of the year, finishing on the 12th of December 1978 in Japan after 77 performances.

David was back to his old distanced self; he was not helped by the **"mountains of blow"** that were available backstage, which also contributed to simmering tensions amongst the members of the entourage. David Bowie seemed troubled to some of those around him, going through the motions; but happy? It seems not.

Perhaps, too, he was burdened with the responsibilities of running his own musical empire. Even before the tour ended, he had released a live album, Stage, which critics complained was too similar to the recordings on the original albums from which they came. It also lacked a live concert atmosphere. Nonetheless, the album went to number 5 in the UK charts although it languished at number 44 in America.

By this time, David was working on another album intended to become the third in what later was dubbed the Berlin Trilogy and which David at the time rather pretentiously called his triptychs.

The experimentation that Brian Eno tried to impose on the musicians at the beginning was abandoned as a step too far, but there were other games to play; switching instruments, for example, or the use of cards with cryptic sayings to spur creative thinking. Unusually for Bowie, he would stop the experimentation extending too far by homing in on ideas that he wanted to have solidified. The album was not brought to life as easily as the others had been and Bowie mused that **"... this had a lot to do with my being distracted by personal events in my life".**

The album was not really a brother to Low and

Heroes; there were no instrumentals and it tended more towards intellectual pop experimentation with strands of new wave and world music, abandoning the depths of its predecessors. In general it deals with the themes of travel and western civilisation. When it was released in March 1979, the album, Lodger, received poor reviews and although it got to number 4 in the UK charts it was not a great commercial success. Expert opinion now, however, considers it to be one of David Bowie's most underrated albums.

This period in David's life was pointing to the end of his time in Berlin, but one of the lasting results of his time there would be a political re-education from German left-wing intellectuals, who finally seemed to be able to deflect him from his fascination with the fascist ethic.

The year also brought David into the headlines in April when what started out as a happy reunion with Lou Reed ended up in a fracas. Guitarist in the Lou Reed band Chuck Hammer, recalled the evening. Reed and Bowie had been discussing Reed's forthcoming album and David agreed that he would be interested in producing the album but only on the condition that Reed stopped drinking and cleaned up his act.

Whereupon the incensed Lou Reed slapped Bowie twice around the head.

"It should be noted", Hammer continued, *"that this verbal bantering also continued into the night back at the hotel — with Bowie in the hallway demanding that Reed "come out and fight like a man". Eventually it all quietened down as Lou never reappeared to continue the fight, and was most likely already fast asleep."*

Bowie would later ask Hammer to play on his next album. Let's not wonder why.

There was trouble with Iggy Pop, too, later in the year; he was losing his musical drive and beginning to float on a cloud of alcohol and dope. Bowie and Coco tried to help him; it was a difficult task.

And this was also the year when the period of experimentation in Berlin would come to an end. It was time for Bowie to move on. There were new challenges ahead, challenges that not even he knew were just around the corner.

ABOVE: Earl's Court, London during his 1978 world tour

SO THIS IS SUCCESS

Concerned with achieving commercial success, Bowie went into the studio in February 1980 to start work on what would emerge as the album Scary Monsters (And Super Creeps). Recording took place in New York, a sure sign that the Berlin years were now in the past. He mostly dispensed with the experimental approach of the Berlin Trilogy and apart from the contribution of guitarist Chuck Hammer, whose guitar synthesiser added musical layers of experimentation encouraged and inspired by Bowie, the singer spent more time developing his ideas by himself, in a more conventional fashion. These ideas contained a sense of existential desperation.

"Scary monsters, super creeps keep me running, running scared

*She asked me to stay
and I stole her room
She asked for my love
and I gave her a dangerous mind
Now she's stupid in the street
and she can't socialise..."*

Many of the original song titles had changed by the time the album appeared. The album was released in September, but a single was released one month prior to that, 'Ashes to Ashes'; it's lush musical phrases with the guitar synth of Chuck Hammer took it to number 1 in the UK, and the album then followed suit. Many people considered it to be the last great work by the chameleon artist David Bowie. Tony Visconti felt it was a high point, too, though he would not work with Bowie again for twenty years.

The singer had taken another momentous decision. He would appear on the American stage in The Elephant Man. Here, at last, David Bowie could show to the world how he felt as an outsider, removed from the society that floated around him. And here, too, was a chance to prove that he was a 'serious' artist; and he took his work seriously. From all the accounts of his fellow actors, gone was the egocentric singer, and in his place came the actor eager to learn who impressed those around him. The review from Variety, said it all:

"... Bowie displays the ability to project a complex character... Bowie shows a mastery of movement and of vocal projection. Bowie takes the stage with authority to create a stirring performance... Judging from his sensitive projection of this part, Bowie has the chance to achieve legit stardom..."

The singer must have felt an incredible surge of contented achievement and acceptance.

And that is how it would have stayed were it not for the assassination of John Lennon in December, an act that frightened Bowie and left him feeling as though a chunk of himself had been torn away. His own mortality was staring him in the face.

Soon, there was a bodyguard trained to kill at his side, and after a brief period for quiet reflection in Switzerland with his son Zowie – who now remembers those days near Lake Geneva in Switzerland as giving him some of his **"fondest memories"** – when Bowie's renewed isolation led him to sense that making friends was not something that came naturally to him, he sought professional help about how to deal with the revved-up lifestyle that he now owned.

RIGHT: Bowie attends the opening of 'The Elephant Man' on September 28, 1980 at the Booth Theater in New York City

81

SO THIS IS SUCCESS

BOWIE STARCHILD

This moment of confrontation with the past, continued as David and Angie went to court to hammer out the terms of a divorce settlement. There was detestation and bitterness on both sides and Angie's access to her son was curtailed. There was also a ten-year gagging order attached to the $700,000 settlement for Angie.

There was a high point in October 1981, when David got together with Freddie Mercury and they released the single Under Pressure, which became a huge hit.

Encouraged by his reception in The Elephant Man, Bowie we had been thinking about another foray into the acting world; a production of Berthold Brecht's Baal. It seemed an apt choice for David Bowie — the work of a playwright renowned for his 'alienation effect', a way of reminding audiences that they were observing actors in the play and not reality. Baal is a drunken womaniser, a disillusioned poet whose dissolute life, as he strikes out at all around him, spirals downwards to murder. No wonder Bowie felt intrigued.

Once again Bowie knuckled down to his task for the TV version; once again a bubble of secrecy was thrown over the project with everyone ordered not to reveal that Bowie was taking part. A sign that Bowie had not quite escaped his paranoid demons. Bowie also recorded the songs for the play alongside producer Tony Visconti. Some of them were recorded in Berlin, where he took the Brecht expert Dominic Muldowney on a tour of his old stomping grounds in the gay and transvestite bars. The EP of the show's music went up to number 21 in the UK album charts in 1982, and the show was generally well received; he made everyone else look as though they were acting, wrote the Guardian reviewer.

Now with the bit between his teeth, Bowie accepted a role in another film that would eventually be titled Merry Christmas Mr. Lawrence. The film shows the lives of British soldiers in a Japanese POW camp during World War I, and Bowie plays Major Jack Celliers, a soldier's soldier, who is sent to a camp in Java, Indonesia in 1942 as a prisoner of war. The film is also an examination of homosexuality and sensuality amongst men in a prisoner of war camp. As one reviewer mentioned, you are always aware that you are watching David Bowie; he brings the same otherworldly characteristic to his role that he employed in his other projects. But he fleshes out the role of Celliers, infusing the major with life. It's one of his finest performances and it was the pinnacle of David Bowie's acting career. When the

ABOVE: Performing on his Serious Moonlight Tour, 1983

BOWIE STARCHILD

ABOVE: Bowie performs on stage on the Serious Moonlight Tour at Feijenoord Stadion, de Kuip, Rotterdam, Netherlands, 25th June 1983

A SPACE ODDITY

film was released in April 1983, however, the film flopped at the box office.

The filming had taken place in England, and the close proximity to his mother also brought David closer to her resentment at what she felt was her son's neglect. Bowie was saved from adverse publicity emanating from her, by Ken Pitt, but not even he could stop David's aunt Pat from creating derogatory headlines in the press. The 'Ice man' tag appeared, unfairly, as David was known for acts of unselfish kindness despite his reputation for being self-centred. Away from the heat of the public gaze and the need to produce, he drew closer to himself, the interested artist always willing to learn from anyone, a true sign of creative maturity.

From the intensity of filming, David went to the intensity of the recording studio again to produce Let's Dance, his fifteenth studio album, on which work began in December 1982. This time, Bowie had engaged Nile Rodgers, American producer and guitarist with the band Chic. This caused a rift with Tony Visconti, who had set aside time for Bowie's project only to be summarily dismissed before recording began.

In a break with tradition, Bowie recorded demos for three days before cutting the album — apparently, Bowie told Rodgers that he wanted the album to sound like Little Richard — and then they finished the whole project in seventeen days including the mixing. Rodgers was almost given carte blanche to bring in ideas and bring Bowie's demos up to scratch musically, and Bowie added vocals only. The singer took Rodgers out and about, trying to feed images into his co-producer's mind hoping they would seep through into the album.

"I've never worked with an artist like that before, said Rodgers, *"... like treasure hunters..."*.

By the time of the release in April 1983, Bowie had joined EMI for a reported $17.5 million. The result was dance pop/rock funk that surprised Bowie by selling 10.7 million copies, his best-selling album.

The only sour note was that Carlos Alomar had refused to work on the album having, as he put it, been offered an embarrassing fee. The reviews ranged from describing this as his best work ever to dismissing the album as "plastic soul work outs. Three of the tracks, **"Let's Dance"**, **"China Girl"** and **"Modern Love"** did become international pop hits, however. Although there were signs that Bowie was sliding into a songwriting cul de sac, **"Let's Dance"** nonetheless sailed up to number 1 in the UK. It was Bowie's most mainstream album to date that seemed to be following the tracks of others, despite always vowing to eschew them.

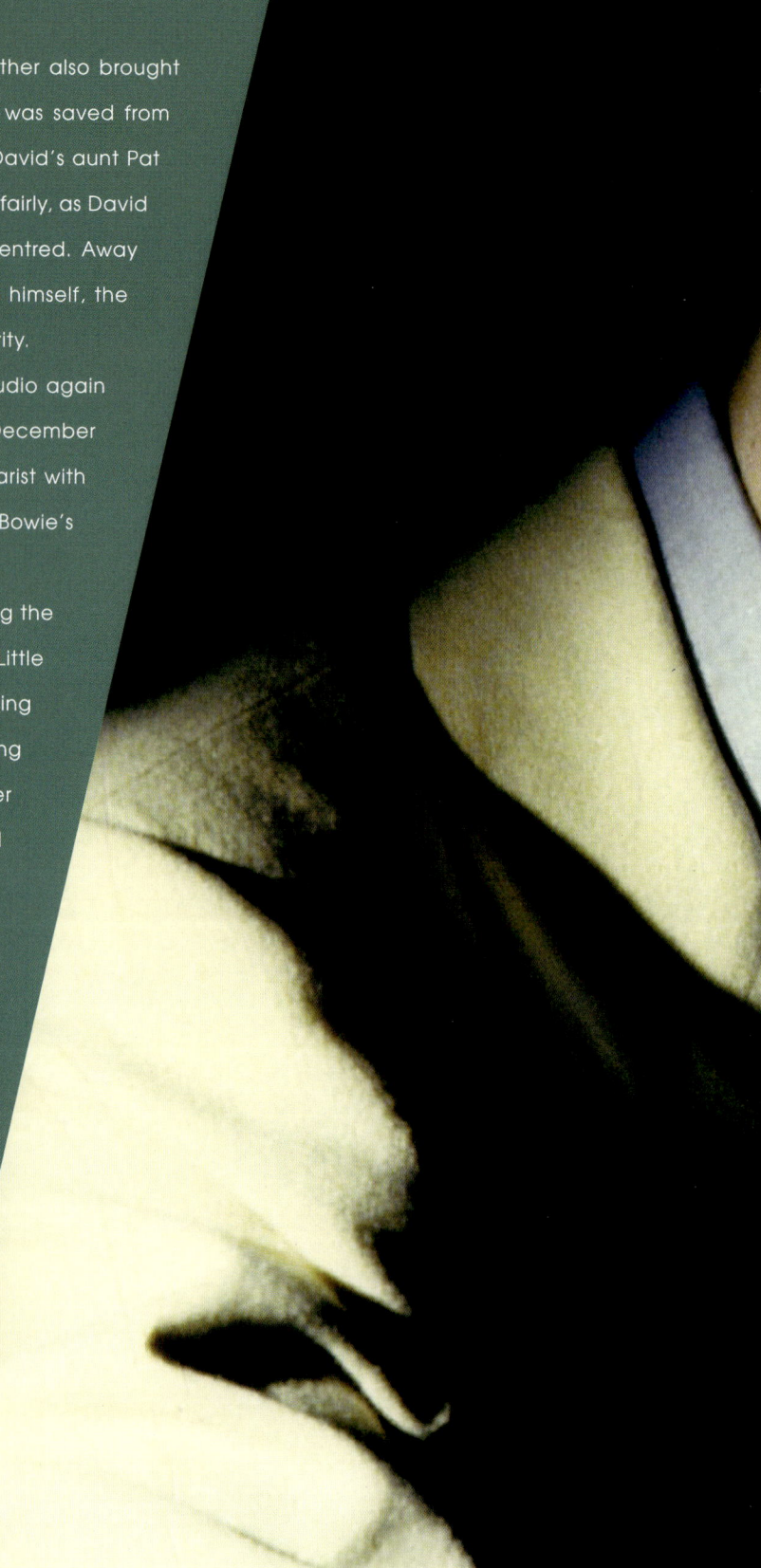

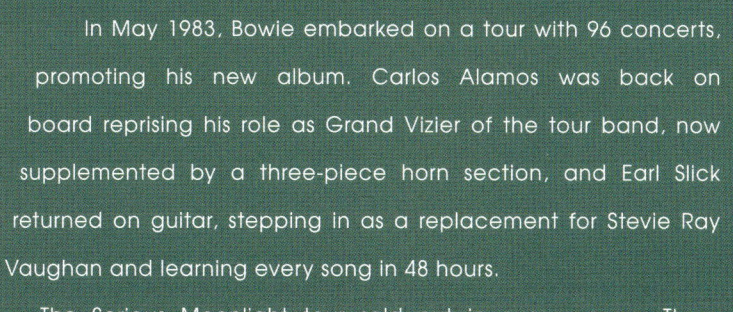

In May 1983, Bowie embarked on a tour with 96 concerts, promoting his new album. Carlos Alamos was back on board reprising his role as Grand Vizier of the tour band, now supplemented by a three-piece horn section, and Earl Slick returned on guitar, stepping in as a replacement for Stevie Ray Vaughan and learning every song in 48 hours.

The Serious Moonlight tour sold out in every venue. There were few props, few costumes, and suddenly, Bowie found himself a commercial success. Many of the great and good came to his concerts and excitement in the enormous arenas was palpable with David on scintillating form, vocally and in his movements.

David's personal life had received an all too brief shot in the arm, too, thanks to his new girlfriend Geeling Ng, who had been a waitress in New Zealand when Bowie used her in his **"China Girl"** video. When she was present on the tour a sense of ease and happiness descended. But Geeling, although only 23 years old, understood the rules of the game and escaped the music world madness back to New Zealand and sanity. That video changed her life, opened a million doors, as she said, and made her a celebrity.

David, it seems, comforted by Coco once any other girls had departed, managed to keep his demons under control most of the time with just the occasional jaunt down the cocaine road, coping well with the pressure of stardom. But the gigantic size of the spectacular tour served only to divorce everyone from the reality of life as the rock-star lifestyle kicked in once again.

In order to keep his hand in, as Bowie described it, he began work on another album designed to sweep in the new fans he had acquired through Let's Dance. Tonight, as it was called, tried to retain the pop feel of its predecessor and once again, Bowie delegated the creation of the music almost exclusively to the band, confining his input to being involved with the vocals. Iggy Pop was back on the scene, too, and remembered that he ***"... worked extensively on that album"***, which meant that he spent a great deal of time in the studio. Two of the songs, in fact, 'Neighbourhood Threat', and the title song 'Tonight', were covers of Iggy's own songs. Bowie refrained from experimentation. What he was searching for this time was a particular kind of sound that he felt he had come closest to achieving in the track

LEFT: Performing on his Serious Moonlight Tour, 1983

BOWIE STARCHILD

"Dancing with the Big Boys".

The reviewers were, as so often in the past, rather lukewarm to disappointed about the album, and even Bowie had to finally confess that it wasn't one of his best, even though it had taken him five weeks in the studio to record, which, he commented, was a long time for him. By now, though, reviewers were getting used to Bowie's 1980s inconsistency. One reviewer, in fact, called it one of the weakest Bowie albums ever. Still, it achieved what Bowie and the record company wanted, which was commercial success, as it rose up to hit the number 1 spot in the UK. Bowie had also helped Tina Turner to secure a contract with Capitol records and the pair duetted in reggae style on 'Tonight'.

But the album's contents seem to reflect what those in the studio had noticed; Bowie seemed simply bored, more interested in I Ching than the sessions, and more interested in looking for women than anything else. It was as though David was beginning to doubt what he was doing, and his enthusiasm of old seemed to have waned. Only his interest in film was as buoyant as ever, and he engaged the director Julien Temple to help put together a production that would be called Jazzin' for Blue Jean, a twenty-two-minute video short. Bowie plays the socially inept Vic, who, intent on wooing a beautiful girl, tries to impress by saying that he knows her favourite rock star. Bowie also plays the rock star, Screaming Lord Byron, to whom Vic eventually loses his girl.

Bowie takes the opportunity to display the hollowness of rock-star life – **"You conniving, randy, bogus-Oriental old queen! Your record sleeves are better than your songs!"** – and gently satirises himself and the low points of his career.

Considered a great success, Bowie unexpectedly revealed an aptitude for comedy acting, and the single 'Blue Jean' also made it into the top 5. But it seemed as though his life was never destined to bring him ease, and on the 16th of January 1985, his brother Terry went absent from Cane Hill, went to his local train station and lay down on the railway tracks. It was the beginning of another low point in Bowie's life and the newspapers, fed by angry and spiteful words from David's aunt Pat, had a field day. Especially when Terry's famous brother decided not to attend the funeral. It was a tragic end to a sad relationship.

DAVID RETREATED TO LICK HIS WOUNDS IN

LEFT & RIGHT: Scenes from the film 'Absolute Beginners', directed by Julien Temple, UK, May 1985

SWITZERLAND:

He was seduced to re-enter the world when Julien Temple asked him to take a role in his next film, Absolute Beginners. Bowie not only accepted the role, he wrote the title music, too.

Attracted by the 1950s era in which the film was set, an era in which teenagers had a burgeoning awareness of the world around them, Bowie even learned to tap dance for the film. To no avail; it was panned and was a flop; in contrast to the music, which reached number 2 in the UK charts. The musicians, Rick Wakeman was amongst them, had turned up for a recording session with a Mr. X, in keeping with Bowie's renowned secrecy. Many consider that song to be Bowie's last good song in the 1980s, and he himself was excited with what he had produced.

Still unable to resist the call of film, David accepted another role in a musical adventure fantasy film directed by Jim Henson. Most of the main characters were played by puppets, but the evil goblin King, Jareth, was played by David Bowie. It nosedived at the box office at the time and received mixed reviews although it has since developed a cult following.

Iggy benefitted from one of Bowie's best songs in that period, 'Shades' which Bowie wrote whilst producing on Iggy's Blah Blah Blah album and then gave to his friend. The album rewarded Iggy with a top 50 hit, his first, when it was released in November 1986.

Bowie then embarked on recording his ill-fated Never Let Me Down album, which he intended as his return to rock 'n' roll — to **"... re-establish what I used to do, a guitar-oriented album. I think the next album will be even more so."** — but it failed to evolve a cohesive style. The title track was about Bowie's long-standing PA and occasional lover, Coco Schwab. Writing the songs — in Switzerland with Iggy — and making the recording, took three months. On its release it was the same old story, opinion was sharply divided; it was either **"... an inspired and brilliantly crafted work"**, or **"... the noisiest, sloppiest Bowie album ever... sad to say, Never Let Me Down is also something of a mess"**. Bowie's reputation took a battering.

Instead of taking the hint, Bowie went into overdrive for the subsequent Glass Spider tour. Not wanting to leave expert hands to do the organisation, he suddenly began interfering in the tiniest

SO THIS IS SUCCESS

Enchanting!

Dazzling! K

detail, wrenching control from everyone else and constantly in a state of high tension. 86 dates throughout the world would take Bowie, his band and dancers, through from May to November 1987 on a commercially successful, but critically derided tour. Nor were people enamoured when they heard that a Coca-Cola sponsorship deal was involved; it seemed that the fans' anti-establishment hero had sold-out to commercialism.

The set was a giant spider, and the show was going to be, **"... ultra-theatrical, a combination of music, theater, and rock"**, according to the star. Overkill and overload seemed to be the most used words when describing the show, which was certainly spectacular, with Bowie even describing it as the most fun tour that he had ever been on.

A contrast, then, to reports that the star was blaming the band for the poor reviews.

No one was sad to see the back of the tour when November arrived. It had, though, proven that David had hit an impasse; he knew it and it was making him unhappy.

Rescue was at hand, fortunately, in the guise of a project which turned out to be a fork in the road; a collaboration with the dance company La La La Human Steps. 'Intruders at the Palace' was the type of project that would always set fire to Bowie's creativity, and he learned some very complicated steps as he provided a foil to the extraordinarily talented and courageous dancer Louise Lecavalier. This was excitement, this was pushing the boundaries, this was where Bowie loved to be. During this period in summer 1988, David became friendly with the guitarist on the project, Reeves Gabrels, and the two men would sit and discuss David's music for hours and from this friendship would evolve yet another change in Bowie's direction that eventually became the Tin Machine project.

David was excited by the prospect of working in another band, and the four members of Tin Machine — Bowie on lead vocals, electric and acoustic guitars and saxophone, Reeves Gabrels on electric and acoustic guitars and backing vocals, Tony Sales on bass guitar and backing vocals and Hunt Sales on drums, percussion and backing vocals — evolved into a hard-rock group. David was showing the world that he had left commercialism far behind. It was an unvarnished sound, and an angry sounding Bowie was flanked by the pounding bass on one side and with the howling melodies of Gabrel's guitar on the other.

THE BAND SET ABOUT RECORDING THEIR FIRST ALBUM, THE TIN MACHINE, IN AUGUST 1988.

David appeared to be relaxed and happy, and his new girlfriend, Melissa Hurley, who he had met when she was a dancer on the Glass Spider tour, had not a little to do with that. Coco Schwab had now been all but forgotten.

LEFT: Scene from the film 'Absolute Beginners', directed by Julien Temple, UK, May 1985

BOWIE STARCHILD

The album was released in May 1989 to generally favourable reviews; *"... **the buoyant Sales brothers and Gabrels certainly equal and frequently surpass Bowie**"*, and although it reached number 3 in the UK charts, it fell away quickly and had sold just 200,000 copies by 1991. A small tour in low key venues was organised to promote the record.

The band never moved away from its rough and ready style of playing together; perhaps, for Bowie, that was one of its greatest assets. He was desperate to avoid anything that sounded conventional, anything that could connect him with what he perceived to be his failures of the past years. He had wanted to be part of a democratic band, without really wanting to be democratic, and the result of his stardom was that much was credited to him for which the other band members deserved the credit. Still, despite increasing tensions within the band, plans were already being laid for further work for Tin Machine.

"I'm so up on this I want to go and start recording the next album tomorrow", enthused Bowie.

Sensing that his old enthusiasm was returning, Bowie had been planning a tour that would present his greatest hits. Visiting five continents in seven months during 1990, clocking up one hundred and eight performances in twenty-seven countries, the Sound + Vision tour, with superb choreography by Édouard Lock of La La La Human Steps, was Bowie saying goodbye to his back catalogue, and he stated his desire to look forward to a new era after the rather dismal perception that had hung over a good portion of the 80s for him.

He began preparations for the tour, rehearsing on Manhattan's West Side. The songs chosen to be performed would then be compiled from a list after fans had phoned in to say which were their favourite tracks.

For Bowie and the musicians the tour was a mixed bag for different reasons; for David after 18 years of touring, revisiting the old songs didn't seem particularly exciting. He was certainly enjoying himself, more relaxed than in previous years, despite splitting up with Melissa. But the musicians found themselves to be subservient to the visual requirements of the set, and a break mid-set for the sponsor's message – yes, David could never quite square the circle of wanting to be an outsider and also an insider – made any musical tension deflate like a soufflé so that audience enthusiasm waned.

The shows on this, David's last large-scale tour, drew a varied selection of reviews that ranged from *"... **Bowie hasn't sounded this good in years**"* to describing the musical clips as *"**stunning**"* or the music as *"**mechanical**"*.

But shortly after the tour finished on the 29th of September 1990, David's life was` about to be changed forever.

LEFT: Performing live onstage on Glass Spider tour, singing into phone, November 1987

CROSSING THE LINE

Her father had been Somali ambassador to Saudi Arabia and she had studied at Nairobi University before a photographer had spotted her and propelled her into a glamorous and lucrative modelling career. Her name was Iman Mohamed Abdulmajid, and she and David had already been introduced in LA before they met again in October 1990.

"I was not ready for a relationship. Definitely, I didn't want to get into a relationship with somebody like him", Iman would say later about their first meetings. David, on the other hand, was overwhelmed, thinking about children's names when they met again on that October night. From that point on, it was clear that their lives would be spent together. Even though, apparently, Iman turned down David's first proposal of marriage in Paris. In the hiatus after the tour, David and Iman spent several months in Los Angeles together as 1990 turned into 1991, and then Bowie became anxious to relive the raw enthusiasm he had felt during the first Tin Machine sessions. The band started making new recordings in March, and their next album, Tin Machine II, was due to be released on September the 2nd 1991. A press event to promote them said that they were *"the future of rock 'n' roll"*; well, not quite.

The tour took off around the world, David accompanied by Iman, and it finished in February 1992.

David was happy to spend his time offstage wandering round museums or local antique shops, and he was also happy to talk about his past to his band mates, and become emotional after a tipple or two from the hotel minibar. It was only natural that having fallen in love for real, with all the emotional upheaval that brings with it, he was now beginning to look forward and backwards across the span of his life and trying to orient himself in his own biography.

Reviews upon the release of the album were less than enthusiastic; *"... well-conceived and well-executed"*, although in 2010, Uncut magazine called it extraordinary. It was felt in later years that criticism of the album had been unduly harsh at the time. It made number 23 in the UK charts and some of the other uncoupled singles also went into the Top 30.

The problem was that the band no longer had the power and urgency in their playing that had set them apart on the first tour. They were beginning to sound conventional. And there were new kids on the block who were hungry and urgent; Nirvana's Nevermind

RIGHT: David Bowie and Iman, 1990

CROSSING THE LINE

BOWIE STARCHILD

was about to hit an unsuspecting world. David never wanted to be old hat. The inevitable happened; Tin Machine was put away on the shelf.

David Bowie had no regrets about his time with the band; they had charged him up, he said later, *"... I can't tell you how much. Reeves shook me out of my doldrums, pointed me at some kind of light — said, 'Be adventurous again'. I've been finding my voice, and a certain authority, ever since"*.

HE WOULD, HE SAID LOOK BACK ON THAT TIME WITH GREAT FONDNESS.

How he would look back on the night he knelt down on one knee on stage and spoke the Lord's prayer during the memorial concert for Freddie Mercury in 1992, we shall never know. He had played the chameleon for so long, that no one really knew when he was being sincere and when he was feeding his image. Perhaps Bowie had one eye on what was about to happen next.

Without a doubt, the most sincere moment of his entire life came on the 24th of April 1992 when he and Iman got married in Florence in Italy, the happy day captured by Hello! Magazine.

Now a happily married man, David set about his next album. He wanted to create a monument to mark the occasion of his marriage to Iman and what better way to do it than with his music. It was to be called Black Tie White Noise and was David Bowie showing that he was moving into the 90s and a new phase of experimentation; it was in fact, the sound of his career being resurrected.

Black Tie White Noise was a mixture of influences with a mixture of emotional content and it was also the last time that guitarist Mick Ronson and Bowie would work together, because David's old sparring partner was to die of cancer on the 30th of April that year.

The song, 'The Wedding', of course, was the tribute to David's marriage, and there were songs about the death of his brother Terence, riots in LA, and a cover

RIGHT: On stage during his Sound And Vision Tour in 1990

or 'Night Flights' by the Walker Brothers. Bowie's voice was strong and his confidence shone through, saving the album, along with producer Nile Rodgers, from what could have been a rather faceless musical amalgam.

Light-hearted and relaxed, David entered the recording sessions and showed glimpses of his old, inventive creativity. Rodgers noticed that Bowie was getting real enjoyment from making his music, and the producer loved the fact that working with Bowie meant never knowing what was going to happen next, and they wanted to see if they could *"... establish a new kind of melodic form of house."*

David picked up his saxophone a lot during the recording sessions, and as even he confessed that he was hardly the greatest saxophonist in the world, his producer was in two minds about this aspect of the recordings; but he went along with it anyway.

David commented that his emotional state was very different at the time; that time brought maturity, a diminishing need to control his inner life and a more relaxed attitude in relating to other people.

"My God, it's been uphill", he said, adding, *"I feel a lot freer these days to be able to talk about myself and about what's happened to me, because I've been able to face it. For many years, everything was always blocked out... I never wanted to return to examine anything that I did particularly. But the stakes have changed. I feel alive, in a real sense..."*

Iman and his marriage had acted as a catalyst, and forced David to analyse what he wanted, what was important to him, what his feelings were, where he wanted to go.

The album went in at number 1 after two weeks in the UK charts. The reviews were good, on the whole; Rolling Stone magazine called the album *"... one of the smartest records of a very smart career"*, although it would have been surprising if there had not been dissenting voices. Entertainment Weekly used the words 'listless' and 'tired' to describe it. Despite it meteoric rise, Black Tie White Noise was not long for the limelight.

So, a musical renaissance had taken place, and in many senses a personal renaissance, too, but even though Mick Ronson had worked on Bowie's last album, the singer refused to take part in the memorial event for the guitarist. It was an omission that left many of the singer's admirers shaking their heads. Perhaps there had been lingering antagonism between the two; perhaps Bowie was in two minds about the guitarist's indispensable creativity and musical contributions to Bowie albums. He certainly tried to *"realign"* history in his favour when asked about the relationship years later. It was a sad ending to a duet that had produced beautiful music, and it showed that David's contradictions had survived the renaissance.

David always relied on a musical compatriot to whom he could throw ideas and from whom he would receive them in return. His next muse came in the form of Hanif Kureishi, the novelist and writer of The Buddha of Suburbia, a book about Kureishi's own upbringing. David needed to be asked only once to write the music for the forthcoming BBC film based on the book.

AND DAVID CAME UP TRUMPS.

Working with a small budget and in a very short space of time, he worked from 10 in the morning until 8 o'clock at night with multi-instrumentalist Erdal Kizilcay. It took only six days to write and record, and as had happened so often in the past, Bowie created something special almost without thinking about it. Whereas David acted as a musical Wizard of Oz, a great deal of the album was created by Erdal and his improvisations that came from ideas and musical sequences discussed between the two of them.

An album was released on the 8th of November 1993 following six months of recording between June and September. It contained a reworking of the film soundtrack and only the title track remained the same; the other pieces were very different. David once described it as his favourite album, and yet its release hardly caused a ripple, being the first in twenty-two years that had failed to enter the charts.

It hardly mattered; by now David was leading the life of a wealthy jetsetter, travelling between his homes in Los Angeles, Lausanne and Mustique with Iman by his side.

But he couldn't stay away from the recording studio for long, and in 1994 he joined forces with Brian Eno and Reeve Gabrels once more; there was a new album to be made.

In what was an unusually long gestation period for Bowie, which stretched from May 1994 until February 1995, the musicians — including long-time favourite Carlos Alomar — were submerged in Brian Eno's role cards, designed to shake up their thinking, and conversations with Bowie, which were designed to immerse everyone's thoughts in the musical experiments. Not everyone felt comfortable with this art-house method of working.

"The narrative and the stories are not the content — the content is the spaces in between the linear bits", said Bowie. Bowie wrote the songs in the studio alongside the improvising musicians.

When the album, Outside, was finally released, on the 26th of September 1995, David had to rework the tracks to fit in with the expectations of his record company. It was a concept album of the industrial rock genre, considered by the reviewers to be either bold and fascinating, or pretentious and almost tuneless. The music fared better than the **"smart"**, **"effective,"** lyrics; "**... a potent collection of avant-garage riffs and rhythm notions"**. And yet, in a pattern that constantly repeated itself in Bowie's music, the magazine Live! pronounced after his death that, **"... pilloried by some at the time for its perceived self-indulgence, Outside will be now be re-evaluated and be found to be one of his very best."**

Oh well, better late than never, and strong praise indeed, proving, perhaps, that David Bowie was ahead of his time.

RIGHT: Performing a duet with Annie Lennox at the Freddie Mercury Tribute Concert for AIDS Awareness, Wembley Stadium, London, 20th April 1992

CROSSING THE LINE

BOWIE STARCHILD

100

ABOVE: Performing at Wembley Arena, 1995

RIGHT: Shoreline Amphitheater in Mountain View California, October 21st, 1995

101

CROSSING THE LINE

Bowie went out on tour from late 1995 to early 1996, devoid of all the paraphernalia and flamboyance of the earlier tours. The band Nine Inch Nails were with him on what had been named The Outside Tour.

The new year of 1996 began with an ending, the end of the European leg of the Outside Tour. There was also an award to make David happy; he was given a Brit Award for his Outstanding Contribution to British Music. He had won the Brit Award for Best British Male Vocalist in 1984. Perhaps it was this acknowledgement by the musical establishment that made David feel that he needed to change the game again if he wasn't going to suffer the indignity of being called lame, as he approached the end of the century.

Gabrels had written a set of electronic music tracks, and soon he was back in the studio with Bowie recording on the hard disk of a computer, and they were excited by this new digital world. It opened up new directions for them, freed their minds of what had gone before, and with speedy decisions, the songs flowed and the album, Earthling, was completed in three weeks. Ironically, the album was criticised for following current musical trends and it did Bowie no favours. It polarised opinion, which was normal for him. This was some of his *"finest music in a decade"*, and he was given credit for encapsulating *"the mood of contemporary popular culture"*. But the album didn't present anything new, and sounded as though the beats had been simply superimposed onto some fairly conventional Bowie songs and sent off with the requisite production values. As one reviewer said, it was simply an *"admirable effort"*.

Bowie turned 50 on the 8th of January 1997, and celebrated the occasion with a birthday concert at New York's Madison Square Garden.

From May of that year he intended to tour for the Earthling album and that would fill up the remainder of 1997.

David was settling into domestic life well, had acquired a smooth and well-groomed American look; he was no longer the cutting edge of musical innovation. He was also accumulating huge amounts of money. And one of the ways that he made money, USD $55 million, in fact, was to sell what became known as Bowie Bonds, asset-backed securities. He sold bonds based on the royalties that he would make on the records he owned made between 1969 and 1990; and this was part of the reason he wanted the money, to buy back the master tapes of his work from Tony Defries. So part of the $55 million flowed into Defries' coffers and everybody was happy again.

Bowie and Iman decided to sell the house in Switzerland and buy a holiday home on Bermuda. Although he had considered his heart was in London, Bowie preferred the anonymity of New York, which is where he would set up home for the rest of his life.

RIGHT: The Astoria, London, 1999

CROSSING THE LINE

103

THE GODS ARE HUMAN

For Bowie, there were three more albums to be made before his life would dramatically change once more. He released Hours in 1999, Heathen in 2002, and Reality in 2003. Hours proved that David Bowie's interest in the internet was not only theoretical; he was astute enough to know that the digital future would bring dramatic and painful changes for musicians, that music would be on tap, like water. On the 21st of September 1999, Hours became the first complete album that a major artist had allowed to be downloaded over the internet. Generally considered to be Bowie musing on the ephemeral nature of life, it was an uninspired album that was heavily criticised in some sections of the music press, and it failed to make the US top 40, the first of Bowie's albums to have suffered this fate since 1972, though it made it to number 5 in the UK thanks to slick marketing.

And so David Bowie slipped into the year 2000, which was to prove momentous outside of the musical sphere. It was a good year; GQ dubbed him the most stylish man of the year, and it was the year he would be nominated for an MTV movie award for his cameo role in Zoolander. It was the year he appeared at the Glastonbury Festival. But the crowning glory came on the 15th of August with the birth of Alexandria Zahra Jones in New York.

David scaled back his musical endeavours then settled into life as a father, determined not to make the same mistakes with Lexi as he had with his son Duncan. His own childhood receded even further into the past with the death of his mother Margaret on the 2nd of April 2001. His father Haywood had died in 1969 and Terry was dead; David Bowie was now on his own.

When he teamed up with producer Tony Visconti again for his 2002 album Heathen, he was back in everyone's good books, and the album went to number 14 in the UK charts. There was even an appearance by Pete Townshend of The Who. Recording had begun in 2000 and continued through to January 2002, so the attacks on the Twin Towers of 2001 had an influence on the album's concept. One reviewer pointed out that Bowie seemed relaxed on the album, had jettisoned the laments about ageing and was now accepting of his situation. It was thought

RIGHT: Bowie rehearsing for The Concert for New York City to benefit the victims of the World Trade Center disaster at Madison Square Garden in New York City. October 20, 2001

105

THE GODS ARE HUMAN

BOWIE STARCHILD

ABOVE: Performing At The Tweeter Centre, Boston, USA 2002

to be a good album, albeit with bleak visions, and although it seemed that he would never reach the heights he had scaled in his early days, he was at least producing work far superior to many younger bands, with 'Slow Burn' being singled out as the best of his original material on the album.

Bowie was now 55 years old and he described this production as *"... a deeply questioning album"*, born from a sense of anxiety that living in America had brought him.

The sense of angst, probably heightened by the birth of Zahra, continued after the Heathen tour and through into his 2003 album Reality.

"There's nothing to rely on any more", said Bowie when talking about the album. *"No knowledge, only interpretation of those facts that we seem to be inundated with on a daily basis."*

Generally well received, the album would be remembered more for what happened on the promotional tour than anything else. Bowie was in Germany backstage at a gig in Prague in 2004 when he began to get pains in his arm and shoulder. What he thought was a trapped nerve turned out to be life threatening. He collapsed backstage in Scheeßel in Germany and was rushed to hospital for emergency surgery on a blocked coronary artery.

For Bowie, it was the beginning of the end phase; he had been searching for a magical way to escape pop stardom and his own dependence on it. Now it had dramatically presented itself to him.

The hubbub and media circus that had surrounded him went quiet as he withdrew from stage and public life, and public appearances were rare. Reports mentioned that Bowie was fed up with the music industry, and he certainly made no moves to re-enter its orbit. Having invested great amounts of time and money to get noticed, Bowie now seemed equally as keen to maintain anonymity, and in his last years tried fiercely to guard his newfound privacy. Permission to photograph Lexi was rarely given.

What no one knew during those years was that Bowie suffered another five heart attacks. Hardly surprising, then, that he enforced a premature retirement on himself.

And then, in 2013, although still a recluse, the years of silence were broken with the announcement that a new album was on the way.

The Next Day was released on the singer's 66th birthday, the 8th of January. NDA's had ensured that the whole project remained top-secret. It was an album of observations that covered a wide spectrum of themes.

Praise was almost universal: It was described with the words 'bold' and 'beautiful', or *"thought-provoking, strange, and filled with great songs"*. This was a *"... celebration of Bowie's own past, swaggering and direct, crammed with echoes and motifs"*, said the Telegraph. It was even described as *"Bowie's twilight masterpiece"*. Kulturnews in Germany ranked it as the second best album of 2013, and it received a nomination for the 2013 Mercury Prize, for Best Rock Album at the Grammy awards in 2014 and for British Album of the Year at the Brit Awards the same year. In the UK it went to number 1.

RIGHT: 2005 Portrait

109

THE GODS ARE HUMAN

It was in 2014 that Bowie became the oldest recipient of a Brit Award for Best British Male, which was collected on his behalf by Kate Moss.

Bowie, it seemed, was returning from his self-imposed exile for on the 12th of December 2015, his musical, Lazarus, opened in New York. He composed the music and lyrics in what was intended to be a sequel to The Man Who Fell to Earth. So hopes were high that Bowie's music would start to flow once again.

And those hopes were not dashed; there were reports that he was busy writing songs for a Broadway musical based on the SpongeBob Square Pants cartoons. And then came the announcement that another album was being released. It was called Blackstar and was released on the 8th of January 2016 the singer's 69th birthday.

The album was a commercial and critical success. It was heralded as *"... a defining statement"*, and Rolling Stone flamboyantly called it *"... a ricochet of textural eccentricity and pic torial-shrapnel writing"*. The album was lush and strange, jazz infused, and did not yield up its treasures at first listening. This was Bowie way out on his own branch again, if not on his own tree, investigating spirituality, death and fame. One reviewer said that he was well and truly *"... back from beyond"*. The tragic irony of those words would soon become all too clear.

The fans rejoiced, but it was a false dawn — because what no one knew was that David Bowie was dying. With his customary intense secrecy, almost no one knew that he was suffering from terminal cancer.

TWO DAYS LATER HE WAS DEAD.

The music had died, the circus tent had been taken down, the starman had gone. One of the 20th century's most famous artists, the mercurial chameleon who had done more to influence the musical culture of his age than almost anyone, had left the stage quietly and unnoticed. The man who had given generations of young people the encouragement to aim above the restrictions of their environment, to take risks and embrace change, who had exercised a life-changing influence on many people, who had opened up a more colourful world, had handed over the creative torch. His constant metamorphoses were templates for performers like Madonna and Lady Gaga. David Bowie was a star and an icon; an outsider whose personal journey was filled with sorrow, pain and excitement, frustration and confusion and finally true love. His lyrics are filled with yearning, alienation and angst. But because of that, the emotional content of his words and the messages they contain will remain to provoke and give courage to generations of listeners yet to come.

RIGHT: Lorde performs with members of David Bowie's touring band at the BRIT Awards 2016 at The O2 Arena on February 24, 2016 in London

111

THE GODS ARE HUMAN

P9762

P9763